BELIEF AND THE COUNTER CULTURE

Books by ROBERT A. EVANS
Published by THE WESTMINSTER PRESS

Belief and the Counter Culture
The Future of Philosophical Theology, Ed.

BELIEF AND THE COUNTER CULTURE

A Guide to Constructive Confrontation

by Robert A. Evans

THE WESTMINSTER PRESS
Philadelphia

Copyright © MCMLXXI The Westminster Press

ISBN 0-664-24939-6

Library of Congress Catalog Card No. 74-165015

Published by The Westminster Press®
Philadelphia, Pennsylvania

Printed in the United States of America

To Mellinda and Judith.
May they share the fruits
of the Emerging Culture with Joy.

Contents

List of Prints and Posters

Foreword

A culture gap looms between two opposing forces. The challenge comes from those persons who are attempting to shape another way of living, an alternate life-style. They are advocating a counter culture. Their impetus comes from a new belief in what it means to be human. Many persons, particularly the young, are drawn to support this challenge. Others, while acknowledging some problems, wish to defend the basic values and traditions of the dominant culture.

It is increasingly difficult to get out of the line of fire. The neutral zone is disappearing. As we seem forced to take one side or the other, that of the Establishment or that of the dissenter, the breach in communication widens. Is there any option except to carry out the duel, to bring the confrontation to a climax? There is a desperate need to avoid a destructive confrontation that will lead to further polarization and alienation. Communication between the opposing parties must be initiated.

A national Task Force on Youth was created. Just prior to the publication of this work, the report *Youth and the Establishment* was released. A portion of this document declares:

Among the conditions for building a working alliance [i.e., "a working relationship based on a modicum of mutual trust without which no two persons or groups can collaborate, however intense their common interests may be"] between youth and the establishment, two stand out as most relevant. The first is the need to take *at face value* what each side states to be its most worrisome reservation, however trivial, irrelevant, or irrational it may appear to the other side. The second key condition is that structured opportunities must be created to permit the mistrust on both sides to be "worked through." There must be opportunities for participants to engage in prolonged encounters, to give vent to strong feelings of anger and mistrust, to overreact, to backslide even after agreements have been reached, to voice anxieties and hidden fears, and generally to undergo the full sequence of experiences involved in reaching conflict resolution. (Daniel Yankelovich, Inc., *Youth and the Establishment*, A Report on Research for John D. Rockefeller, 3d, and the Task Force on Youth, p. 87. The J. D. R., 3d, Fund, Inc., 1971.)

In light of the crisis in communication, the purpose of this work is to offer a bridge across the culture gap. Here is a possible medium for contact between people who reside at different levels of consciousness, who have divergent visions of this society and of themselves. The intent is not to bring them necessarily or initially into agreement, but rather into meaningful conversation. In the face of the crisis described, this "package" proposes several means by which some members of these divergent groups could be drawn into constructive, even therapeutic, involvement, conflict, and, I hope, authentic communication. Such an experiential dialogue assumes a basic interest and goodwill on the part of each party.

This work took shape not primarily out of theoretical reflections and study, but rather through experiential encounters throughout the country with people of all ages and vocations struggling with the problems of communication and understanding across the culture gap. We engaged one another at rock festivals and in church parlors, at experimental communes and in college classrooms, at love-ins and political rallies.

The project was given its particular form by twelve study seminars composed of fifteen people in the post-thirty range and fifteen younger persons primarily in their late teens and early twenties. The seminars were held in representative geographical areas ranging from California to New York and Alabama to Michigan. Included in the samples were urban, suburban, and semi-rural settings. The aim was to discover peoples' emerging problems, visions, and dreams and to help in their struggle to find a common language and a unifying vision. Thus my reflections are not an attempt to fabricate a vision or prophesy a cultural revolution (both of which would be pretentious and futile). Rather, I am seeking to identify, articulate, and perhaps sensitize others to a vision that is already taking shape and to draw attention to a cultural shift of which we can already feel the vibrations. I am describing my own observations and intuitions and do not claim to be comprehensive.

One conviction that arises partially out of an intuition of the emerging culture is that this is not the age of the traditional book. The emerging culture is much more an eye- than an ear-oriented phenomenon. It is my judgment, therefore, that a multisensory rather than a purely verbal presentation is more likely to achieve the desired purpose. This package involves not only a written text but also directions for a simulation game, recordings of original folk music, that incorporates themes from the counter culture, prints that satirize not only "straight" society but the counter culture, and reproductions of poster art, which has been described as "the cave art of the twentieth century." Also included is a Guide with specific suggestions for initiating such an experiential encounter with various groups who have an essential interest in cultural change. Such an encounter could be sponsored by church groups, service clubs, civic and school organizations, or even by a group of friends concerned with this problem of a so-called generation gap or a cultural revolution.

The book might be usefully employed as a resource for each member participating in the study seminar. However, it has also been designed for use by a seminar leader who is skilled in group work and who is acquainted with the motifs and experiences of the counter culture.

The concept of "constructive confrontation" will have significance only if it becomes a communal and experiential reality. This package of collected catalytic data is intended to be used in a small group of twenty to thirty persons in which different perspectives on the culture gap are represented. The intent is not to project a normative perspective into the scene, but to provide a structure and a means whereby genuine communication may occur.

My debts for BELIEF AND THE COUNTER CULTURE are more to persons and experiences than to books. However, numerous written sources stimulated my own reflection and proposed ideas that later became incorporated into this work. I want specifically to acknowledge Theodore Roszak's The Making of a Counter Culture and Michael Novak's *The Experience of Nothingness*, which first articulated trends I had been encountering. *The Greening of America*, by Charles A. Reich, came to my attention after the basic ideas had been formulated and the project launched, but it served to confirm and connect my judgments.

To my students I give a great vote of thanks for their "great refusal" to accept ideas that did not touch their human existence. Thus they challenged my life-style and humanity and initiated my own personal quest for the humane and the holy. This quest was supported and facilitated by special friends in the "family group."

This work attempts to avoid the use of technical, philosophical, and theological language. For those who are interested, I have argued the case theologically for a "transformation of consciousness" in *The Future of Philosophical Theology* and have repeated and restated a part of that argument in the pages that follow. Also, a detailed philosophical consideration of symbolic communication is contained in *Responsible and Intelligible Talk About God,* soon to be published.

BELIEF AND THE COUNTER CULTURE is for the general reader. The constructive confrontation it seeks to evoke was actually experienced by a number of groups. The text and particularly the Guide were modified as a result of the experiences and evaluations of these groups. To the persons who gave their time, energy, and, most of all, themselves, I am grateful. The initial experimental seminars were sponsored by: Presbyterian Church of Western Springs, Western Springs, Illinois; Central Presbyterian Church, New York City, New York; Yorktown Heights Presbyterian Church, Yorktown Heights, New York; Southminster Presbyterian Church, Tulsa, Oklahoma; Germonds Presbyterian Church, New City, New York; First Presbyterian Church, Lake Forest, Illinois; The Winnetka Presbyterian Church, Winnetka, Illinois; Fairfield Presbyterian Church, Fairfield, California; First Presbyterian Church, Napa, California; Napa Covenant Presbyterian Church, Napa, California; First Presbyterian Church, Vallejo, California; Community Presbyterian Church, Vallejo, California; First Presbyterian Church, Auburn, Alabama; Presbyterian University Center, Auburn University; The Episcopal Church of the Epiphany, Houston, Texas; Continuing Education Seminars of Oklahoma-Arkansas Synod; Community Presbyterian Church, Big Rapids, Michigan.

The often painful stage of manuscript revisions would not have been passed without the insightful queries of the staff of The Westminster Press, Trudy Priester, and Larry Rasmussen. Their labors are appreciated, but clearly they cannot be held responsible for the final result. Mary Lee Reed entertained the children (first things first), reviewed the manuscript, and endured typing marathons. Diane Schiltz, Ernstine Ware, Deanette Small, and Meredith Spangler typed portions of the manuscript when it took the form of lectures for courses or alumni meetings of McCormick Theological Seminary.

The greatest debt is to my wife, Alice, who serves as resident artist and editor, critic, and comforter. She has suffered through my own transformation of consciousness and shared in the struggle to fashion a new life-style. More than anyone else, she has embodied for me the transforming symbols of love and peace.

R. A. E.

Chicago, Illinois

1

Visions and Dreams

Your sons and your daughters shall prophesy,
   your old men shall dream dreams,
   and your young men shall see visions.

(Joel 2:28.)

There is a revolution coming. It will not be like revolutions of the past. It will originate with the individual and with the culture, and it will change the political structure only as its final act. It will not require violence to succeed, and it cannot be successfully resisted by violence. . . . This is the revolution of the new generation.[1]

A cultural crisis is upon us. With this assessment, both young and old agree. We are on the brink of a revolution. Yet the nature and purpose of this revolution is unclear. Certainly not all see the revolution as a renewal of America. Many understand what they see emerging, not as a "greening of America," but rather as a defoliation of American culture.

This crisis involves uncertainty about the future, lack of clarity about priorities, doubts about our value system, and confusion about our life-style. The present unrest has not been produced by the young, but it certainly has been proclaimed by them. It has therefore come to be known as a youth revolution or a counter culture, but in actuality it involves us all. To ignore or dismiss this revolution, to fail to recognize emerging life-styles (prevalent among but not confined to the young), not to take seriously the questions about our value system, bodes disaster and a continuance of the crisis in America.

This crisis is a malaise characterized by alienation of person from person and group from group. The President takes as his aim a cry emerging from our people, "Bring us together." And the high school junior declares in growing frustration and disappointment, "If only my parents and teachers listened and understood." So it is the age of "gap talk"—the credibility gap, the economic gap, and, of course, the generation gap. It is the last of these with which I am particularly concerned, for it is this phenomenon which makes the brooding revolution so extensive, so personal, yet so promising.

It is not, however, primarily a matter of age. There are cultural revolutionaries on both sides of the mystical demarcation line—age thirty. Therefore, it is not simply a matter of a generation gap, but rather what I prefer to call a "culture gap." Culture is used here to designate "the concepts, habits, skills, arts, instruments, and institutions of a given people in a given period."[2] Culture implies a person's view of the world, his vision of reality. The crisis of our culture is not fundamentally the result of an age differential, but rather a vision differential. There are those within our society who have radically different expectations, hopes, and commitments about the shape of our society and therefore about themselves. The problem or the potential is often characterized in terms of the young versus the old, the rebels against the knights, or the dissenters against the Establishment. This I believe is due to a difference in vision, not in genealogy.

We are on the brink of a major shift in culture that may be comparable in magnitude and pervasiveness to the Renaissance or the Reformation. Perhaps it may be prophesied in just these terms. This "new Renaissance" is characterized by a new birth in aesthetic sensitivity. There is a consuming and expansive interest in new forms of art, literature, and music. Also, there is a revival of interest in authentic learning. It is focused, not on the monkish scholasticism of most lecture- and book-oriented educational institutions, but rather on an experiential encounter with a wide spectrum of persons, communities, and material that results in a mind-expanding awareness—an ever-expanding awareness of one's self and one's environment.

We are also on the eve of a new cultural transformation that might be regarded as a "new Reformation." It is described in precisely these terms by Paul Goodman because it shall result in "an upheaval of belief that is of religious depth, but that does *not* involve destroying the common faith, but to purge and reform it."[3] This new cultural experience will elevate the issues of value, authenticity, and direction of human life. The foundation for this cultural transformation will rest on a man's belief, his faith, what he trusts and commits himself to in such a way that it integrates and revitalizes his life.

Would a tantalizing image for this new emerging culture be a marriage between a new Renaissance and a new Reformation? For the two merge and become one at the point of their common concern and obsession—What does it mean to be human? Perhaps one could best symbolize this cultural upheaval as a "rehumanization" of culture which has at its core the universal question of belief.

One might inquire: What are the persuasive signs that we are teetering on the brink of such a cultural explosion? How could these indices of cultural revision be understood as any more than a temporary offshoot from the mainstream of culture? This visionary revolution, some may proclaim, is only a meandering stream that departs from the main river and wanders joyously, noisily splashing along and experimenting with new territory. It returns eventually, however, to the mainstream, providing it with fresh water and new impetus but driving on in the same direction. On the contrary, I am convinced that what we are experiencing may better be compared with a river that has been gorged by torrential rains. It is inadequately banked and at the same time is so dammed and clogged with debris that a gigantic flood results, a new tributary is formed which cuts its own fresh bed out of the earth, and it finally becomes a new river. It will never return to the old stream bed, but, having bypassed the old blocked channel, finds such freer areas in which to expand that the water of the original channel finally comes tumbling turbulently but gratefully into the new opening. The tributary has become the mainstream.

To follow this analogy and consider the status of our present mainstream of culture, data could be amassed about the present crisis in communication, intimacy, and authenticity. The elements in this crisis can be understood as pointing to a growing tendency, although by no means the victory, of the dehumanizing processes in our culture. Consider the catalog of death-producing wars, the increasingly debilitating search to find a liberating and humane economic process, and a personal life-style that suppresses authenticity and restricts one from obtaining genuine community. But these judgments could be considered argumentative and abstract. Let me point only to a factor that I observe in human experience and let the confirmation rest experientially with the reader. A kind of restlessness and uncertainty verging on despair is evidenced in every facet of our culture once it is exposed to examination. It is perhaps best expressed in the relationship between parents and their children or between teachers and students, and even employers and young employees. Just a few years ago when the college-age members of society expressed rebellious doubts about the meaningfulness and direction of our culture, they were often encouraged and supported by parents to take time off for a summer's work in a new locale or even a "junior year abroad" to gain perspective. This meant in rather implicit terms that students could be as experientially free and revolutionary as they desired as long as this was experienced in some location other than home ground. The correct assumption for the most part was that those same young persons would eventually return to take up the same kind of job, live in a comparable home, and with a life-style similar to that of their parents. The disconcerting phenomenon of our present experience which is continuing to grow is that many of the young are refusing even to accept this calculated "time off." They reject not only the values and life-styles that have become predominant in our culture but even the validity of the reasons that supposedly undergird such a life-style. They are not about to assume even under the most intense pressure an existence with un-

fulfilling work and the dehumanizing communal relations that they now perceive to be operative. The factor most indicative of the cultural shift is that now many parents not only understand this rejection but also have a disturbing suspicion that their offspring are correct. However, in the midst of this apprehension many parents with no vision for an option, an alternative, become defensive and caustic. This reaction affirms the judgment of their younger critics.

In your mind's eye picture a man in dingy blue burdened as if a huge boulder were strapped upon his back. Clutched in his hands are volumes of written matter that have been consumed but have not enlightened. His eyes are weary but searching. To one side, others gesture and jeer at his agony and his foolish quest. He is driven but not drawn; seemingly possessed but not obsessed. He seeks illumination; he finds only explication.

The print included here by Robert Hodgell provided the catalyst for this mental mirage. One might be perplexed by the imposition of the seemingly pious query, What shall I do to be saved? If one takes the word "salvation" to mean "wholeness" or "healing," as it was sometimes employed by Paul Tillich, then the pilgrim's query not only manifests the religious depth of the pending cultural reformation but becomes a cultural question as well. It becomes at its core a human question. What shall I do to be more alive, authentic, fulfilled, and therefore human?

Is this perhaps a shadow image of our times, resting just beneath the surface of consciousness for us all? The image of a person searching frantically for a vision that will transform his life, yet finding in frustration only justification and explanation for the way things are? This figure hides in each of us but may be apprehended in the professional man or student who

PILGRIM BEGINS HIS JOURNEY

This print is available from Robert Hodgell, Box 46813, Pass-a-Grille Beach, Florida 33741

gives up on the political system as intractable and retreats to private life or his technical studies. Consider also the member of the church or synagogue, the religious man who abandons the religious institution because it is dull and inapplicable to his life, despite fervent protestations about relevance. So our religious institutions deteriorate not only in money and membership but also in momentum.

The Christian church, to direct attention to a particular religious institution, is in trouble today not because it is so controversial, but rather because it is so boring. Too often it does not speak to genuine human issues. It has an "edifice complex" and is obsessed with possession and preservation, to which Hodgell's print satirically alludes. Another illustration involves the serving of the Sacrament of the Lord's Supper, the bread and the wine, which becomes central to the liturgy and life of the Christian church. In most congregations, this act is now accompanied with such solemnity that it would frighten away the Lord himself. It is not celebrated as a life-affirming experience accompanied with joy and a sense of renewal and revitalization. Rather, its power as an illuminating and transforming symbol to integrate human life has been suppressed if not destroyed.

A parallel case emerges in our educational institutions. Some of the most perceptive students are dropping out because they believe the prevailing pedagogy, methodology, and criteria of some aspects of their education are petrifying their own sensitivities to what it means to be human. So college unrest in ever-changing forms increases and academic involvement declines despite the fact that our educational institutions at some levels still provide a socially accepted refuge from the draft. A basic problem in education is rooted in a kind of rigidity of style and teaching process that has developed in a society that puts a high priority on advanced formal education. The grading system, set course requirements, and tenure become the basic bastions of the educational *status quo.*

Classroom rigidity and reliance on formal lectures are illustrated in the case of a professor of philosophy of religion in a large American university who was lecturing on one occasion, as all such professors must, on the relationship between predestination and free will. He noticed that one of his students in the front row had not been taking notes of any kind for four consecutive days on a topic upon which the professor had some considerable reputation. After class on the fourth day he could contain himself no longer and he inquired of his student why he had not been taking any notes. The student responded by saying: "Well, professor, I really don't need to. You see, I have my father's."

Our educational policy has such limited perimeters that it has stressed the role of the expert, the transformation of data, and even proper educational methodology to the extent of stultifying not only one's hunger to learn but also genuine creative potential. It is from this present environment of rigidity, classification, and stultifying tradition that the emerging culture seeks to break free and breathe. This growing revolution has at its core a new vision or dream not only of America but of the self.

How, then, would one begin to engage the American society as a whole in this nonviolent revolution, this creation of a new vision, this reshaping of a dream? It must be stressed that one really cares about this new vision for the self and the shaping of a renewed American dream only if it makes a real difference in how he lives, if it affects his values, his commitments, and his expectations. The vision may be dependent on what a man believes in and therefore what he trusts. Perhaps our unrest is linked to an insatiable quest for a guiding illumination, for a transforming vision. Thus before we can respond to the queries: How do we get beyond this crisis? and What is the future of our nation and our people? we must deal with a prior, inescapable question. Is the primal concern for a new vision today the justification of present belief or one's liberation for an experience that may result in a transforming belief?

In the future, those who seek to recast our transforming vision (a task often directly assumed by philosophers and even theologians of culture) will not be concerned *primarily* with analysis, explanation, or justification of predominant attitudes, institutions, and practices, nor will they propose means for reforming these elements specifically. Rather, their task will be the discovery and the articulation of a new vision that shall shape even our present understanding of reality.

Certain members of society have historically done the job of explanation and justification with notable competence. Politicians and their supporters vindicate present position and procedures, teachers defend basic method and content, business executives interpret company policy, parents justify and explain traditional mores. We have all profited from this effort, and most of the persons who function within the institutions of the society have contributed directly or indirectly to this task. However, sometimes the quest for cultural conformity and clarity has appeared to result in triviality. We have analyzed, dissected, qualified, and reduced not only our language about the goals of self and nation but even about God himself. The mystery is eroded, the vision is corroded until the nation and God, or rather our experience of them, succumb, and the nation's collapse and God's demise are not only the result of a thousand qualifi-cations but the impoverishment of a vision by which man lived.

We must take care not to fabricate our guiding visions wildly and irresponsibly lest we construct castles in which no one can live. One of the pitfalls for the emerging culture is the tendency to design just such a castle that no one can enter because it lacks a drawbridge to cross the moat. However, neither dare one make the building specifications on any cultural dwelling so rigorous and so rigidly enforced that the only option is to build a kennel in which no one wants to live. So we remain at the stage of examining blueprints because it does not seem possible or desirable to build under the present conditions. Yet we want and need a place in which to live and from which to go out into the world and return. What we lack is the vision of a viable structure and a means to circumvent the established building code. We will seek a vision from an architect who is more creative than the technocrat. If we cannot discover that vision or a means of negotiating the specifications, we shall revolt against the building authority and reject present requirements as absurd and repressive. In the words of Theodore Roszak, as he tries to articulate the insight of many young people who glimpse a vision of the future and seek to develop a more authentic life-style for themselves, "We should reject the small souls who know only how to be correct, and cleave to the great who know how to be wise."[4]

The present malaise prods us to ask if it is not time to look in a new direction beyond justification, explanation, and mere renovation to consider another option. The student cries out in response, "What we need first is a change in consciousness." From students particularly, but not exclusively, comes the urgent plea for a vision of life that really affects a person's life-

FOR HE HAD GREAT POSSESSIONS

This print is available from Robert Hodgell, Box 46813, Pass-a-Grille Beach, Florida 33741

style, a world view about which one could conceivably, in the words of posters plastered on subway cars and student doors, "Give a Damn!"

What does this new mind-set involve? This new understanding of reality? The term that I have employed is the transformation of "consciousness." (The term is used here in a wholistic way, comparable to the manner in which it is employed by Charles Reich when he says, "Consciousness . . . is not a set of opinions, information, or values, but a total configuration in any given individual, which makes up his whole perception of reality, his whole world view.")[5] Consciousness in this instance is really a new perspective through which all human experiences are viewed and interpreted.

The transformation of consciousness sought here could result in a vision of the richness, beauty, and capacity for human fulfillment in life. It fashions an alternative image of human identity, human community, and the modes of interaction between man and his world. The consequence of transformation of consciousness is a new sense of reality. This new mode of experiencing is a metamorphosis of one's sensibilities, a transmutation of the valuational criteria, and a new way of adjudging human transactions.

A sensitized soul twitches under the present anxiety and confusion, seeking a new form of consciousness. But even if this new sense of reality is desperately needed, how is a person or a community to formulate, create, or discover this new state? Where does one look for clues to this new life-style? What are the sources or intuitions for the type of engagements or experiences that might result in the reordering of a person's perspective on life? What are the marks of authentic futurity?

The attempt to grapple with these questions will, I think, elucidate the two theses of this work. The first thesis is that if the cultural revolution that is surfacing is to have a future meriting serious attention and scrutiny, it must be involved with a change in consciousness that does in fact alter one's life-style. The second thesis is that the most fruitful place to look for clues to this radical change in consciousness is in the instinctively correct intuitions of what has come to be called the counter culture and forms the catalyst for what I also wish to call the emerging culture. This latter thesis may "blow your mind" because it runs counter to the dominant culture's assessment of the so-called youth culture and its depiction in mass media. However, Theodore Roszak, who has made one of the most comprehensive efforts to identify the characteristic motifs of this culture, confirms my judgment when he suggests that this fragile, indistinct vision of the future is one of the few things "we have to hold against the final consolidation of a technocratic totalitarianism in which we shall find ourselves ingeniously adapted to an existence wholly estranged from everything that has ever made the life of man an interesting [and I would add a humane and holy] adventure."[6]

The present crisis is a result of the gradual surfacing of this new image of what it means to be human, of what it means to be a member of a community with shared priorities and goals even in the midst of plurality and diversity. This process is revolutionary because the young are proposing a vision of what it is to be human that is in conflict with the generally accepted image of the society. This posing of an alternative vision is often associated with the counter culture, since it seeks radically to transform the American image.

It should be noted that the cultural revolution I am describing is fundamentally apolitical. This is particularly important if one tends to associate with the counter culture a form of radical

BELIEF AND THE COUNTER CULTURE

political action that takes violence as one of its instrumental options. It is quite clear that violence is incompatible with the new vision of humanity that is being expressed by this emerging culture. If one takes a recent campus or even capitol bombing as a symbol of the thrust of radical political action, it is instructive to reflect on the witticism that notes that such a bombing has as much connection with changing the world as an obscene phone call has to the rape of the Sabine women.[7] In recent gatherings of those who declare themselves to be a part of or at least associated with the counter culture, anyone advocating publicly the violent overthrow of the government often has been booed right off the stage. There is a new mood among those convinced that we must change the mind-set and priorities of the nation. This is particularly evident on the campus. The restlessness of the past has taken a new form, and many of the more perceptive students are examining their own personal priorities, the question of the relationship between self and society, and are attempting to discover what patterns of life-style and action would in fact change the essential nature of our culture. Their conclusions appear to have neither a political nor a violent character. My own concern is with a cultural revolution that is not in the first instance political. However, a new perspective on reality and society would of necessity have political implications at some later stage.

Therefore, in considering the dimensions of this essentially cultural revolution, we must qualify, focus, and charter the term "counter culture." It has sometimes, particularly in the mass media, been used to encompass, and on occasion come to be identified with, political radicals who see violent revolution as *the* means to transform society. This association is now repudiated by the very nature of the movement, as is so beautifully illustrated in the music of Kathy Gregory, "After Cambodia," included in this package. It was precisely "After Cambodia" that the contradiction between violent, coercive methods of any kind and the integrity of the cultural revolution became evident. To identify counter culture with political activity is inappropriate, and with a radicalism that urges instrumental violence is clearly wrong.

"Counter culture," like the term "youth culture," also can be deceptive if it is identified primarily with drug culture, a genesis in rock music, experimentation in communal living situations, or distinctive forms of dress. This identification has been fostered of late particularly by the mass media and is ironically symbolized in the decision of *Time, Life, Newsweek,* and major newspapers to accept "counterculture" as a common noun fundamentally characterized by these more sensational and "news engaging" traits. Not only is this a form of misrepresentation, as the media exploits the more bizarre aspects of this cultural revolution, but, more significant, it is fundamentally superficial.

One consequence of the implicit co-option of this culture by popularizing its dress, language, and music is the demeaning of its symbolic importance. The more foundational issue for the counter culture is that of transformation of consciousness, a new vision. This new consciousness may become exhibited on occasion by appreciation of or experimentation with dress, drugs, or rock. But what has been too frequently ignored is the positive commitment to a new style of living that evidences what it means to be authentically human, joyously alive, and personally fulfilled. The fundamental and authentic motifs of the counter culture involve priority of experience, creativity, symbolic communication, communality, and an openness to the transcendent that bring about a transformation of consciousness. This new consciousness may be expressed in rather experimental and superficial fads, but the primary concern is the consciousness of itself. If these foundations of one's life and action—these motifs which structure one's existence—are included in one's understanding of the term "counter culture," then it is applicable. It will be employed here as two separate words not only to symbolize a resistance to superficial co-option of this cultural revolution but also to emphasize its more permanent, contributive, and transformational potential. Thus a more penetrating analysis of counter culture involves this new vision of what it means to be human. It can, therefore, be understood not only as a "counter" culture but also authentically as an "emerging" culture. It is not only culturally destructive but also constructive. It seeks not only to blot out one image but also to build up another. It seeks at its core to disrupt only in order to reconstruct. The dawn of the emerging culture is not only a time when our sons and daughters shall prophesy (we should recall that prophets in any age are unwelcome, particularly in the church and university), it is not only a time when young men shall see visions, but it is also a time when old men shall dream dreams. Surely we are on the verge of a cultural revolution that encompasses us all. Let us then, young and old alike, take it as our task to create a vision of renewal and not deterioriation. In order for prophecy to be received, visions understood, and dreams interpreted, we must have a medium of communication of which we are presently devoid. A means of opening up new levels of conversation is imperative to the realization of the dream.

The task of fashioning, adjusting, and implementing a new vision awaits. Yet an integral factor in the present cultural crisis is the absence of effective channels of communication. There is throughout our culture a crisis in communication or what has been described as a "crisis in intimacy." While many of the young have been concentrating on how to "turn on" to life, persons at all age levels have apparently learned how to "turn off" each other. There is an inability genuinely to hear and authentically to understand what a man with another perspective is saying. Words flow in and out without making contact, and everything becomes a matter of "my opinion." But probably more indicative of this crisis, there is an increasing unwillingness to risk one's self in sustained encounter in order to discover what another is saying, to comprehend and evaluate it. It is undeniable that there is a desperate need to develop lines of communication between the young and the old, between those who wish to call into question the values, style, and direction of our culture and those who find themselves part of that culture and therefore defenders of it. The yearning, however, is not for another analysis of the problem from either side of the culture gap, no matter how insightful. Rather, there is a desire for a means to span this chasm between the rebels and the knights.

The crisis in communication is symbolically represented in the story of a Puerto Rican woman who lives in New York City (it could just as well have been any large metropolitan area). The woman learned one morning that her husband had been arrested for vagrancy when he was out on the street seeking a job. He had been unemployed then for some weeks. On hearing this news from a neighbor, she frantically rushed from her apartment in order to communicate with her husband at the local precinct headquarters. The nearest phone was in a bar located on the bottom floor of her apartment house. She rushed in and telephoned the local precinct. The police sergeant on the phone was brisk and efficient. He informed her that he

IN MY OPINION

This print is available from Robert Hodgell, Box 46813, Pass-a-Grille Beach, Florida 33741

could not provide her with any additional information until the proper forms had been processed in reference to her husband. The woman, nearly hysterical, began to lapse more and more into Spanish. The police sergeant was unable to understand her and in frustration finally hung up. In increasing panic, the woman proceeded to plead with the men in the bar to assist her in finding out when her husband would be released. Her fear caused her now to plead rather wildly and therefore to lapse naturally into her native tongue. The men in the bar were unwilling and incapable of understanding her. Thus the bartender finally called the police, and the woman, now in genuine panic, was taken to the psychiatric ward of a large city hospital. Two days later a social worker who spoke Spanish was contacted to visit the woman. A few minutes after this conversation had commenced, it was learned that this frightened woman was forced to leave two tiny babies alone in her apartment. When they reached the apartment, authorities found both children dead. Because no one took the time or interest to understand, because communication was cut off only for a short period—death resulted. This story has a word to say symbolically to our culture. The impediment to communication here was fear and frustration, which forced the woman to retreat to her native language. But are the consequences of our crisis in communication so much different? The threatening nature of our assertion, the resulting defensiveness, the difference in perspective—in consciousness, if you will—make our situation comparable to that of being divided by a foreign tongue. And so death bodes menacingly over us as well—not a physical death immediately, but rather a spiritual or visional death. We must find ways to reestablish communication. The purpose of this work is to supply some suggestive catalytic material in order to initiate significant communication between people with different perspectives, with different consciousnesses of themselves and of their culture. This work provides some guidelines for such a cross-consciousness dialogue. My intent is to offer some provocative interpretation and to suggest an agenda for constructive confrontation between the Establishment and the dissenters.

"Confrontation" is a word that has been captured by the politicized radical groups. The term may therefore immediately evoke either attractive or repellent images. The word "confrontation" has become so politicized that it is refreshing to find it satirized as it is in an event reported in the German magazine *Der Spiegel:*

After students of Wadham College in Oxford University had presented their faculty with demands in the form of ultimata, the instructors responded by letter as follows:

"Dear Gentlemen:

"We take note of your threat that, should your demands not be accepted immediately, you will initiate what you label 'direct actions.' We think it only fair to let you know that to our faculty belong: 3 experts in chemical warfare; 1 former member of the commando troops who is experienced in explosives and the torture of prisoners; 4 sharpshooters in pistols and rifles; 2 ex-members of the artillery; 1 bearer of the Victoria Cross; 4 experts in karate; and 1 chaplain. We look forward to what you call a 'confrontation' with confidence and await it with pleasure."[8]

However, the irony of this satire is that it may characterize the predominant tendency to respond to the threat of immediate encounter rather then to the fundamental issues that precipitate the threat.

It is important to observe that historically Americans thrive on confrontation. In a recent address Michael Novak observed that there resides in our history a frontier image projected into contemporary life that calls for a quick shoot-out. So the myth reads that in the streets of our emerging frontier culture any point of serious disagreement could be settled immediately in a showdown. There would be no pussyfooting or delay. The question of right or wrong, of who ought to wear the white hat or the black hat, could be instantly resolved by an encounter in the streets. Thus students are encouraged by one another to confront the faculty. The faculty members are urged by society and boards of directors to stand up to students. Workers are urged to put management to the test, and the managerial force wants an immediate strike or no-strike decision. In foreign affairs the most satisfactory resolution takes a form comparable to the Cuban missile crisis and not the prolonged agony of a Korean truce. Thus in recent years it has appeared that many people are running around like mad looking for someone to confront. We have in other words a fantasy about quick confrontation and resolution, and to sidestep a confrontation is somehow thought to be un-American. There is perhaps one sense in which that is true, for an encounter between parent and child, teacher and student, employer and employee, which ends in either one stomping from the room is perhaps a refutation of a certain frontier courageousness. Each party must be willing to lock horns at least for a sufficient amount of time to hear the other's point of view and attempt some form of common communication.

However, I would suggest that there are constructive as well as destructive forms of confrontation. This work strives to implement constructive confrontation, by which I mean a significant and sustained encounter between persons of divergent viewpoints concerning crucial issues for their style of life. Constructive confrontation involves essential conflict, since it concerns those things which are at the very core of our being, our expectations, and our hopes. It demands immediate encounter and communication but not instant resolution. It is based on the presupposition that sustained involvement with the intent to understand results in new insight. A constructive confrontation cannot be based on accusations from either side of the culture gap that result in hostility and defensiveness. Rather, a sensitive and loving sharing of one another's visions is essential. Such an encounter induces not merely conflict but reconciling struggle. Whether this package can function as this kind of guide for constructive confrontation remains to be seen. However, it depends as much on the motivation of those who are engaged in the confrontation as it does on the adequacy of the bridging mechanism.

It is my hope that this project will be a guide or an instrument for an experiential encounter between those who are struggling to understand one another and thus grasp together a new vision for themselves and for the society.

NOTES

1. Charles A. Reich, *The Greening of America* (Random House, Inc., 1970), p. 4.
2. *Webster's New World Dictionary of the American Language* (The World Publishing Company, 1956), p. 359.
3. Paul Goodman, *The New Reformation* (Random House, Inc., 1970), p. xi.
4. Theodore Roszak, *The Making of a Counter Culture* (Anchor Book, Doubleday & Company, Inc., 1969), p. 238.
5. Reich, *Greening*, p. 14.
6. Roszak, *Counter Culture*, p. xiii.
7. F. X. Shea, S. J., "Reason and the Religion of the Counter-Culture," an address presented to the American Academy of Religion (Boston, 1970).
8. *Der Spiegel*, April 6, 1970, tr. by David Larrimore Holland.

II

Belief and the Prophets

What does the new vision of an emerging culture have to do with belief? In a recent book entitled *Science and Secularity,* Ian Barbour describes a situation that might be elaborated as follows: There was a group of scientists who had been working on a very complex computer for several years. It was a computer that would be able to handle extremely involved and subtle judgments. The task was completed. The cybernetic engineers spent several more months programming the computer with data from all aspects of human experience. Just prior to beginning the serious testing procedures to determine the capabilities of this new computer, the scientists decided, in order to break the growing tension of anticipation, that they would pose a somewhat whimsical, but nevertheless probing, question. So they typed into the machine: "Is there a God?" The huge computer whirred, turned, and then typed out the answer which read, "There is now."[1]

Each of us has in his own way some deity, some ultimate concern that serves to guide, shape, and orient the way in which he leads his life. This is a question then of belief. Belief does in my judgment characterize that which is authentically human. Prof. Schubert M. Ogden, of the University of Chicago, asserts, "To exist as a

self at all is possible solely on the basis of faith [or one might say "belief"], so that the statement, 'Unless you believe, you shall not understand,' is true in a sense not only of the Christian or of the religious believer but of every man simply as such."[2] One's belief or faith, i.e., his confidence in and commitment to the shape of human existence, constitutes the distinctively human quality. If this is so, the focus here must be on belief. It is the contention of this work that the fervent belief and commitment of those who share in the emerging culture express a more humane vision of the self and the society than that of the established culture.

So it is that we begin to unfold the themes and motifs of the emerging culture, with its new vision, its new dream. Thus we explore the beliefs, commitments, and priorities that determine one's understanding of what it means to be human and part of a community. It is impossible to say precisely and comprehensively what it means to be authentically human any more than one can photograph a vision or encapsulate a dream. For being human is not a fixed quality, like the capacity of a computer; but it is always in process, always becoming, like the gradual maturing of a child. The maturation of a child is not a steady process, but it surges ahead and falls back and sometimes appears to be arrested and in retreat altogether. Just so, there is a pendulum effect to maturity, with insights and capabilities recovered and emphasized only to be lost in a balancing swing.

Thus the themes and motifs of this emerging culture are obviously not a totally "new thing under the sun"; rather, they witness to a process of rehumanization or recovery of certain traits and values that had been smothered or neglected. They are distinctively human because they seek to facilitate the recovery of the authentic self in community. In the new culture, one's aim is to expand awareness of self and others, to enrich personal and communal experience, and therefore to become more sensitive, loving, and accepting. This results in a transformed consciousness that makes one more fulfilled, alive, and joyous. It is linked to a new vision of the self and the community. Some of those specific themes and motifs involved in the process of becoming "more human," for which the counter culture cries out, are these:

1. Priority of experience and subjective involvement.
2. Recovery of mystery and restoration of creativity.
3. Concern for communication and the symbolic dimension.
4. Revitalization of community and openness to transcendence.

These themes and motifs will be unpacked, explored, and illustrated in the following chapters. They can become provocative catalysts for dialogue and communication but not finalized goals for cultural development. Even if I am wrong about the cultural revolution and its direction, and even if these goals could be exposed as inauthentic and inadequate, the tasks of confrontation and communication, conflict and reconciliation, are imperative in a responsive and healthy culture. I am convinced, however, that certain of the motifs discussed here can be ignored by society as a whole, and particularly by persons within the church and the synagogue, only at the peril of growing irrelevance and morbidity. Already, sensitive people confess that life neither in the secular world nor in the church and the synagogue speaks to their existential needs. To put it bluntly, we can and must learn from the counter culture. Even if frantic experimentation with life-styles in the emerging culture appears bizarre and superficial, even if the Bohemian young who are publicly identified with the counter culture are often formally, miserably educated (usually at the hands of the dominant culture), even if we are confronted by an "adolescentization" of dissenting thought and culture, still frequently their instincts are freer, more visionary, and instinctively healthier than those of us administering or abetting the technocracy. The lines of conflict are defined as if those of one culture were separated from those of another by the bars of a cage. Yet it is not clear who is imprisoned and who is free.

Some aspects of the newer life-styles may turn out to be mistaken or inauthentic and only signs of adolescent rebellion and frustration—simply a more joyous cop-out than others of us who are frustrated with our existence could manage. Still, I am persuaded by the prevalent unrest and persistent quest for vision among those who align themselves with the emerging culture that theirs are the themes with which educators, philosophers, theologians, social scientists, even politicians in at least the next decade must grapple. Margaret Mead contends that we are on the verge of a period when the young will "prefigure" culture for the rest of society. The day is past when one gained his culture from his elders, "postfigurative." We are nearing the end of the time when one received his culture from his peers, "cofigurative."[3] I doubt that the prefigurative state is upon us yet in the society as a whole and certainly not in the religious institutions, but if one is going to hazard predictions about the future, where is a more likely place to explore than with the young?

The danger in speaking about faith and commitment to the human with a religious dimension is that this becomes just another attempt to be faddish, or worse yet, to co-opt the vitality of the youth movement for the religious establishment. Thus we may have not a commercial but a "religious vulgarization" of the counter culture. There is always the danger of co-opting either the young or the principle of youth. The latter was perhaps epitomized in the years of the Kennedy administration. In that period, to be young (rather broadly and loosely defined) was the fundamental prerequisite not only for a political appointment but for having one's views taken seriously by many in the power structures within the culture. Wisdom and insight became identified with youth and enthusiasm rather than with age and maturity. If a person had not achieved the apex of his profession as defined by the dominant society by the time he was thirty-five, he was unlikely to make it. This trend has been modified in the last several years, but the cumulative consequence of this experience persists. A number of persons who were actually young (in their early twenties) were put in advisory roles and positions of authority in government, education, and even business. The effect was to place an undue and unrealistic burden of responsibility upon the young. They did not possess the experience, maturity, time, or energy to bear the responsibilities that society seemed to attribute to them. The result was not only to produce a splurge of activism particularly within the political realm but also to increase anxiety and a growing burden of guilt. Commercial interests, advertising, and particularly the mass media, manipulated the "youth binge" until the expectation for youthful revolution and change was enormous. But the productive result was minimal. This is best epitomized in the Presidential campaign of McCarthy, which resulted not only in widespread disillusionment and frustration but also in a sense of failure and guilt. Therefore, in reference to the much publicized activities of the young, it is useful to distinguish, I think, between their overt activities and concerns and the insights, authentic motifs, and revitalized symbols that emerge from their experimentation and ring true.

If these themes command consideration, who shares in this emerging culture? How did it arise? And perhaps most significant, what are its implications for one's personal life-style? Is it true that the emerging culture may eventually encompass us all? We look, of course, to the students in the universities and graduate schools who will be the future educators, legislators, financiers, theologians, and philosophers. I am convinced, however, that it would be a mistake to look only or even primarily to the university scene. Several analyses of culture in the past have tended to identify the characteristic interests of the young with those of the highly educated, (or at least thoroughly schooled), middle-class young, in the later years of high school and in college. This has led to a romanticizing of the youth movement and also to a capitalizing on these attitudes in a way that becomes almost faddish. Thus we are warned to avoid either an unduly romantic or a skeptical attitude toward the youth culture.

Who *are* participating in the themes and motifs of the new emerging culture? It is perhaps prudent first to identify those who are not in the vanguard. The overt thrust of the counter culture appears to exclude the conservative young who

BELIEF AND THE COUNTER CULTURE

THE CAGE

This print is available from Robert Hodgell, Box 46813, Pass-a-Grille Beach, Florida 33741

hold down lucrative establishment jobs or are frantically preparing for them in the multiversity. As the president of a large engineering school in the southeast remarked recently: "We don't have much unrest on our campus. The boys are too busy preparing to join the affluent society to have time to fight it." If you are preoccupied with mastering the cybernetic age, you don't want to short-circuit the computer.

A number of recent studies conclude that the majority of those in college today are rather "straight" if not downright conservative in the sense that they have accepted the patterns and values of the dominant society in terms of vocation, political system, and educational process. Many more college and graduate students talk about a radically new life-style than actually live it. The unknown quantity, of course, is what internal processes are going on. Has there been, as I suspect, an attempt by many students to make a temporary truce with the system, both to evaluate it further and still to use it, not cutting off themselves from its benefits during the process? At the same time, a critical examination of priorities by many of the more sensitive collegians may lead to a new assault on the Establishment. This may not be an external and political but rather an internal and spiritual assault, aimed at bringing about a transformation of consciousness.

Militant black youth, and, increasingly, brown and red youth, are not committed to the counter culture, but rather are struggling to reap the benefits of a technocracy that has prospered partially on their exploitation. They do not want initially a changed consciousness as much as a technocracy with more soul in which they have a significant share. A qualification should be noted, since this exclusion of militant blacks is based on their public declarations. The frequent rejection by militant blacks of the thrust of the counter culture is quite understandable in the light of the danger that the white middle class will use the theme of a transformation of consciousness as another way to cop-out on giving racial minorities their due in social, judicial, or economic matters. The pastor of a large black church on the West Coast declares, however, that many of the themes and motifs of the emerging culture are an integral part of the black experience. Some of the themes, such as free expression of emotion, communality, and openness to transcendence are clearly embedded in the black experience. Therefore, one seems impelled to agree with Reich when he declares that "the blacks made a substantial contribution to the origins of the new consciousness."[4] Therefore, once again one must be attuned to distinguish between the articulation of immediate concerns and interests and the empowering motifs that determine the consciousness of the people.

Finally, the politically oriented, whether new left liberal, radical revolutionary, or Marxist organizer, feel estranged from the essential pacificism of the new emerging culture because their hope lies not primarily in a new mind-set but in a transfer of power. The concentration is on learning the techniques and methods of the present political process, of community organization of guerrilla tactics, or of revolutionary propaganda and control. The new revolutionaries are good sons of the technocracy.

In view of all these exclusions one is tempted to ask, Who's left? Is this emerging culture visible anywhere? It is important to make several observations at this point. The first is to reject the kind of theme prominent in mass media that identifies the counter culture or emerging culture with persons who have cut themselves off from the system and are distinguished primarily by dress, drugs, or music. As a corollary, it is significant to note that the new emerging culture has not taken root, so that it can be unmistakably identified with any one group or subculture. This would be to focus only on the rather superficial symptoms of a shifting culture. Actually, the power of this emerging culture is evident as its fundamental themes and motifs become manifest at many different points throughout the culture. A new vision of the human is beginning to take form, even though it has not yet been completely realized in any one location. Attitudes resulting from these motifs are more prevalent among but not confined to the young. When basic presuppositions that determine consciousness are changed, there is a stronger argument for a genuine cultural shift than when certain groups simply polarize around distinctive forms of overt behavior.

However, for this perception to have substance, it would seem necessary to locate the frontiers of this emerging culture. These themes and motifs are cultivated at a depth level among students at various stages in academic life, and they also play an important role within the black experience, although this has not been the major thrust and articulation of the black community up to this point.

Interestingly enough, some of these motifs are overtly manifested not only in those who have separated themselves from the dominant culture in what has come to be called a "hippie" lifestyle but also in a small but evidently growing number of skilled workers who would strongly reject any such label. Note that in 1970 there was a 280 percent rise in applications for the Peace Corps by skilled workers.[5] Though a new ruling allowing spouses and children has certainly affected this increase, a shift in goals must also be considered. These are men who appear to be seeking not only meaningful work but also expansion of experience and adventure. Here, too, perhaps there is among skilled workers a hint of the urge to recover the self.

There are at least two other representative areas where we can see the new emerging culture taking specific form. The first area may be a quite surprising one. And in the absence of fully representative data, I put it in the form of a tutored speculation. The junior highs of our nation, particularly those in urban areas where there is direct contact with minority groups and other subcultures experimenting with divergent life-styles, seem to be a part of the emerging culture. Originally, I had discouraged the participation of junior high young people in study seminars on this topic. This policy was revised when I found it increasingly true that sometimes operating within the junior high range were young people quite perceptive and critical about the inadequacies of their present educational procedures. They were quite open to new forms of life-style and a thorough evaluation of priorities. This could, of course, be the result of an age when one is highly impressionable and therefore open to a number of alternatives. However, it is my judgment that the kinds of cultural revolutionary motifs that are surfacing in the society are really being perceived and embodied by those in lower levels of the educational system because these young people have become more critical of the whole operation and have also had less time to have the standards of the dominant society solidified within their ranks. If this judgment is accurate and we are not simply observing a faddism in vocabulary, dress, and personal action, then the impact of the cultural revolution is much more pervasive than many of us have recognized.

The area that provides the best testimony to a permanent and authentic new direction for our culture is that of the young professionals. It could be argued that what we have represented in the junior high, high school, and college young people is simply continued evidence of an alienated middle-class youth in the process of a rather extended adolescent rebellion. This argument, however, is not basically applicable to the young professionals, many of whom are in their twenties and early thirties. They have experienced not only the frustration of dealing with the dominant culture, but many have affirmed the authenticity of a critique and the freeing potential of the new modes of valuing, acting, and living. In his book entitled *The New Reformation*, Paul Goodman affirms this observation when he notes the important agents of change to be among the professionals and academics who are not only dissenting but diverging from the Establishment.[6] It is just this action which Goodman thinks makes the present movement comparable to the Protestant Reformation. If this is in fact the case, a transformation of consciousness has already occurred, and in fact it is beginning to be implemented with a new life-style. This commitment to a new emerging culture is typified by the young physicians who are turning their backs on private practice and going into public health service in order not only to denounce inadequacies in the present system publically but also to attempt to restructure the form of medical care in public and university hospitals, which is often not only inadequate but actually dehumanizing for those in need of its services. The emphasis here is on preventative medicine, which stresses again the natural functions of the body and the environment.

Let me provide a concrete illustration of this in the case of a young specialist at a large university hospital who had objected to the administrator that his students were allowed to examine only so-called "welfare" cases. Private patients could not be included in the process of a teaching program. He declared to the administrator of the hospital that this distinction was demeaning to welfare patients and thus was ethically questionable. He was told by the director that they were helpless in this matter, since private patients would refuse to be subjects for examination by interns. The doctor found the practice unacceptable, but on the other hand it would benefit nothing for him to resign as he was encouraged to do by one colleague.

The procedure he followed instead was first to approach one of his private patients and ask if he would not prefer to have several very bright and perceptive students with him during an examination. He also noted that it would assist them in the hospital training of new physicians. First one patient agreed, then five, then fifteen, then twenty, and then several of the other private patients began to complain—because they were being attended by only one physician. As a result, the policy of the hospital on this matter was changed.

The most significant factor was an equalization of treatment for all patients in the hospital. The policy change sought to negate a value judgment about human worth in reference to wealth. This perception has been a factor in the rebellion of interns in several hospitals across the country as they demand equitable service and care for all patients. There was in operation here a new kind of life-style that had its implementation in this one specific area.

Another example emerges in the case of a young lawyer who took his degree from a leading school, specialized in tax law, and spent several years working for the government. He discovered that his time was primarily employed in prosecuting persons who had relatively small tax deficiencies, some of these actually made inadvertently. The whole question of tax reform and the large number of corporations that through legal loopholes evade enormous sums of taxation was completely ignored. As a result, he left government service and went into a partnership with a friend who had had a similar experience. Their wives worked in order to allow them to invest their legal expertise in assisting poverty cases as well as organizations that could not readily afford to contract for the lawyers' services. In addition, they organized committees of taxpayers to form lobbies for tax reform in which their expertise was invaluable. In this case, there was a clear decision to forgo the status, the rewards of the consumer system, and normal professional advancement because of a commitment to a meaningful profession which realized some of the human priorities that had become crucial. In this case, it was the implementation of a vision that had been fleetingly discussed a year before and finally there was a commitment to the necessary adjustment to actualize such a vision. The commitment of "Nader's Raiders" may be further confirmation of this whole phenomenon.

A third example is of several young academics who had a growing conviction that the present educational system did not do much more than train a person for a functional role within the established culture, in the process stultifying his imagination and creativity as well as dampening his natural curiosity and love for learning. These young scholars took their own financial resources, much of them obtained through publication, and invested them in the establishment of a free high school and a free university. This school emphasized the experiential background of the student as well as his prior formal education. They eliminated all formal curriculum, requirements, attendance, expectations, and grading procedures. The classes were run on a contractual basis concerning the material that arose from a student's authentic curiosity. The students when they so desired could engage in and be joined by the professor in an evaluative pro-

cess of their educational development. Admission was determined by lot. Admission to the experimental program was so sought after that youngsters were known to weep when the lot did not fall to them; and on occasion the class was actually crashed by other students anxious to discover and share in this educational process. Again, the remuneration, the status, and, one would even have to add, the immediate evaluative satisfactions were virtually eliminated for the young teachers involved.

Each of these three examples is symbolic of the themes and motifs that are empowering young professionals, with dreams of a more humane life and society, to transform not only their professions but their individual life-styles. Their belief in and commitment to a meaningful realization of their human potential in a way that is more experiential, creative, communal, and loving springs from an undergirding vision of what it means to be a fulfilled human being. Here rests not only the evidence for this new emerging culture but also the potential models and paradigms for future transformations.

It is becoming increasingly clear that those identifiable themes or motifs associated with the counter culture are certainly not confined to the young, although the attitudes proposed seem to be most highly publicized here. Ironically enough, the expanded and redefined age boundary of the "youth nation" is fourteen to thirty. And that critical, almost mythical, upper limit will continue to creep up as those who, in some sense, initiated or experienced a change in consciousness continue to age. Thus it will be transformed into a real "counter" culture naming new foundations upon which to build the illuminating and transforming symbols of a culture.

The question of what led to the rise of the counter culture poses a fascinating and complex problem. At the source of this question is the issue of the fundamental need within a society to allow for and encourage the emergence of a new culture and therefore life-style. Both Theodore Roszak in *The Making of a Counter Culture* and Charles A. Reich in *The Greening of America* have attempted to survey at some length the primary factors that have led to the projection of this new cultural dream. The factors are numerous and interrelated and merit more scrutiny than can be undertaken here. If, however, I were to point to *the* symbolic event symptomatic of the need for a new culture, it would be the dropping of the atomic bomb on Hiroshima and Nagasaki, for in this event we have the most tragic but prophetic illustration of the demise of the Western human *intellectus*. If one doubts the utter negation of the humane implicit in this act, one should view a film of the bombing of these two cities which was released in 1970.[7] It shows both the incredible extinguishing of hundreds of thousands of human lives within a matter of seconds, and also the futility not only of the initial bombing of Hiroshima but beyond question that of Nagasaki just a few days later when there was no possibility for the Japanese government to respond in a way that had been politically prescribed. Here was a pronouncement of the utter degradation and worthlessness of humanity, not only of those who were killed but the dehumanization that occurred in the act of destruction itself. Even more sinister is the arbitrary, calloused nature of this act against all mankind. These were not simply isolated acts of war. Rather, they were the result of a series of scientific investigations and political machinations. The suppression of the film for some twenty-five years after this event was a further indication of the fear of those directly responsible for the act for what it in fact declared about the nation and about the world. Acts of war had before, of course, been arbitrary and inhuman. However, the very magnitude of this atrocity screamed out that any notion of a humane *intellectus* was utterly destroyed.

The Vietnam war has reinforced and confirmed this image, and for young people today, epitomizes a militaristic mind-set that is almost incomprehensible to them. As Reich declares, the corporate state could engage in almost any kind of activity, no matter how impoverishing to human life had it not taken the form of a prolonged and publicized war. "The war did what almost nothing else could have: it forced a major breach in consciousness."[8] If the atomic bomb on a more massive scale followed by the Vietnam war in a more limited perspective was a parabolic declaration of the destruction of a significant concept of what it means to be human, then here lies the wellspring of the emerging culture. If every cultural consciousness is, as Reich suggests, a reaction to the one before, then the pendulum swing of a new emerging culture accentuates a concern for persons in their uniqueness, creativity, and inviolability.

Consuming interest in the counter culture is stimulated not simply by multiplying numbers of its followers but even more by what Herbert Marcuse has called "the great refusal." This "refusal" is the rejection not just of national priorities, policy procedures, control of information, and authoritarian organization, but the great refusal of the present human consciousness and the values, communities, and actions that it yields. The counter culture throws an indignant finger in the face of a mind-set that is obsessed with and possessed by a consciousness of objectivity, rationality, individuality, nationality, secularity, and conformity. Even the repetition of the "itys" is as boring as the controlled efficiency of the computer, which has become the paradigm for the modern society. Rooted in American pragmatism, "the vision of a wholly artificial environ-

NO MORE WAR

ment, man and society together restructured by the power of the machine, is the American dream."[9] This is a technocratic vision (if "vision" is an appropriate term) which can kill both physically and spiritually. The new culture, in at least one of its characteristic moods, cries out against this mind-set, "Hell no, we won't go!"—which refers to much more than just the war.

The counter culture considered here, characterized by this revolution, obviously embodies more than just negativism—more than just a refusal to cooperate with a process of dehumanization. There is a new vision taking form which is yet to be fully deciphered, but the major figures are emerging from the shadows. It is the vision of what it means to be human, the gift of a transformed consciousness which emphasizes: experience and subjective involvement, the expression of feeling and recognition of mystery, the sense of community with one's brother and the environment, religious sensitivity and openness to experience of transcendence, the value of joyful undirected creativity. The vision is composed of illuminating and transforming symbols that shape this consciousness. The discovered symbols interact with each other to create a new myth or drama that guides the shaping of a new lifestyle.

The influence of the emerging culture, despite its apparent minority status, is becoming, more and more significant among the young and adult groups. Sometimes it emerges only in the superficial form of dress or lack of it, hair length, and vocabulary selection. There is even the danger of conformity to a new subculture not necessarily more authentic than the one rejected—as Paul Tillich reminds us, everything has a demonic potential. Yet these superficial signs may, I think, be an indication of one's being on the edge of a transformation of consciousness. It is frequently our brightest, most creative, and most sensitive young people in the university, high school, and junior high who not only dress uniquely but express opinions that make the generation gap more than a cliché and play havoc with the expectations of the educational institutions. Yet an authentic "counter" culture would intuit that real transformation must be wholistic. It involves more than a switch in apparel, language, and musical pretense, and form of intoxicating substances consumed. It convinces more and more young people that they must separate themselves altogether from their inherited culture and move into communes or other experiential communities in order to work on the problem of consciousness and provide new models for this visionary future, or as an alternative find creative ways not only to resist an imposed consciousness but to share and implement their dream.

The fact is beginning to dawn even on the young political activists who are submerged and frustrated that not only the key to a "new congress" but to a new nation rests in the sphere of consciousness which is not fundamentally changed by another series of white or black papers or a few more antiwar congressmen. Harold D. Lasswell in his study *Politics: Who Gets What, When, How* declares: "Constituted authority perpetuates itself by shaping the consciences of those who are born within its sphere of control. . . . Hence the great revolutions are in defiance of emotions which have been directed by nurses, teachers, guardians, and parents along 'accredited' channels of conscience."[10] The insight of the counter culture is that you must give priority to a change in consciousness. If we wish to consider "conscience" a product of one's consciousness, then Michael Novak supports a similar point: "In order to take part in a revolution, therefore, a man must first do battle with his own instincts; he must rupture his own conscience."[11] To do this means to expel or at least radically cull the old determinative symbols under which we operate in order to give them a fresh evaluation. Perhaps that is why I like the expression of the youth culture, "blow your mind," because it suggests the initial process in the transformation of consciousness, namely, blowing the mind clear of the old presuppositions. You may wish to restore some of them to their places of priority but they may not gain reentry unexamined. However, the problem in some aspects of the counter culture is that the mind appears to have been blown clean without any replacement.

It should be made clear that there is a "dark side" to the counter culture of which this work gives little explicit account. This includes: a tendency toward faddism and compulsive conformity to a new subculture; and individualism that is basically hedonistic when it is not transformed by communality; a romantic vision of the "natural" that sometimes condones excesses which manipulate rather than support other persons; and, finally, a lack of sensitivity to and acceptance of the visions of those outside the emerging culture which negates the principle of intrinsic human worth. Despite these dangers, I see great *promise* in the basic motifs of the emerging culture and sense the enormity of something huge happening in the consciousness. Thus I have become an enthusiastic advocate of seriously encountering the emerging culture. Justifiable criticism of the counter culture abounds. However, this work hopes to highlight the pervasiveness and promise of the counter culture. The vision of the counter culture is worth the time and immersion in it to check out its import for *every man* and for our society as a whole.

I believe there is a new vision emerging that has not been manufactured of whole cloth as have the advertising images of the good life or the great society created by technocratic culture.

Quite to the contrary, the vision has been discovered or received as a consequence of reactivating sensibilities that were dormant and repressed. The new image of man and of community is coming into existence as a result of man's transaction with a reality not apart from but beyond him. Perhaps one can be so bold as to suggest that the new vision emerges out of an encounter that is in fact between man and God. If this is so, one can even risk interpreting our present crisis as a time when the Spirit of the Lord is being poured out and young men shall see visions and old men (like me) shall dream dreams. We are being summoned to a constructive confrontation, to a sustained encounter across the "culture gap," but we must listen to each other and try to understand. Let us unite for this task with hope and a sustaining commitment to that reality which frees us for a new transforming belief concerning what it means to be human. Belief in this new vision summons us now to expand the horizon of our experience.

NOTES

1. Ian G. Barbour, *Science and Secularity: The Ethnics of Technology* (Harper & Row, Publishers, Inc., 1970), p. 95.
2. Schubert M. Ogden, "The Task of Philosophical Theology," in Robert A. Evans, (ed.), *The Future of Philosophical Theology* (The Westminster Press, 1971), p. 56.
3. Margaret Mead, *Culture and Commitment: A Study of the Generation Gap* (Doubleday & Company, Inc., 1970).
4. Charles A. Reich, *The Greening of America* (Random House, Inc., 1970), p. 222.
5. *Chicago Sun Times*, March 6, 1971, p. 33.
6. Paul Goodman, *The New Reformation* (Random House, Inc., 1970), p. xi.
7. *Hiroshima-Nagasaki, August, 1945* (Center for Mass Communication of Columbia University Press). I am indebted to a colleague, Jack L. Stotts, for this interpretation.
8. Reich, *Greening*, p. 215.
9. Herbert W. Richardson, *Toward an American Theology* (Harper & Row, Publishers, Inc., 1967), p. 28.
10. Harold D. Lasswell, *Politics: Who Gets What, When, How* (Meridian Book, World Publishing Company, 1958), p. 42.
11. Michael Novak, *The Experience of Nothingness* (Harper & Row, Publishers, Inc., 1970), p. 107.

III

The Priority of Experience

Experience is the most precious of all human commodities. It is also becoming the most difficult commodity to acquire. The human capacity to encounter another person, object, or event in a direct and natural way is becoming increasingly rare. If experience is taken to be the actual living through of an event or encounter, a personal engagement with another being, then much of our present society constitutes an assault of the experiential. The aim of a technological society is to provide men with all the commodities they desire, experiential as well as material. We are caught in a substitutionary obsession which provides artificial products in food, clothing, and even grass. (One may take astroturf as the epitome of artificial utilitarianism.) One of the distinctive things about the human is having the capacity for experiencing the expansion of humane awareness. This involves the ability to apprehend, appreciate, and enshrine within one's memory an engagement with another. Therefore, a suppression of the experiential is in fact the suppression of the human—it is a process of dehumanization.

Some analysts of technology have suggested that we are now on the verge of the ultimate step, namely, that of packaging and producing artificial experiences that will involve not only sight and sound but also smell and feel and even movement. The new cultural revolution wants to emphasize the crucial role of experience, but it must be an experience that is direct, natural, and authentic in contrast to the artificially manufactured and packaged experiences toward which the technocratic society is moving. This concern is evidenced by the dramatic renewal of interest in experiential data as well as in addition to that which is logical and theoretical. The emerging culture with its concern for rehumanization takes as one of its most prominent themes the priority of experience—experience that is actual and genuine. Education increasingly involves more field trips and laboratory work. Internships are becoming the order of the day, not only in the professional fields but also in business training. Health foods, with their emphasis on the natural, claim serious attention. There is a trend in clothing to make it less expensive as well as more directly related to the products and colors from which an article is derived. Finally, the enormous interest in ecology is one of the clearest repudiations not only of pollution but also of the whole substitutionary and artificial structure of society.

If a person is struggling to make a judgment or to come to a decision, particularly if this involves a significant factor in his own way of life, what are the primary resources for making a determination and thus a commitment? The emerging culture insists that experience is clearly the point from which to begin and must rate priority as over against theoretical presuppositions or logical argumentation. However, the dominant culture asserts that one should base decisions on logical arguments, and appeals to publicly verifiable evidence. If the latter is the case, then the experience has no real priority, in the sense of cruciality or finality. What the emerging culture asserts we need is not simply a reconsideration of experiential data, significant as that is, but a change in consciousness that appreciates the priority of that data. The pivotal question is not whether experience will play a role, but rather what role that will be and what mode of experience will be central.

A conflict concerning the role of experience in decision-making is illustrated in the following situation. A financially successful suburban businessman involved in one of my seminars stated that he had received a job offer that involved a move. He frankly asserted: "You've got to be realistic. The final decision must be based on my calculation of the possibilities for advancement in the business." His eldest son, a high school junior, expressed his strong opposition to the fact that in this decision neither the experience of the entire family, his feelings, his father's feelings, nor those of the other family members were crucial. The issue here is not simply one of ultimate goals, nor of what choice the father makes. Rather, the focus is on the criteria considered in making the decision. In this instance a son was asking his father to give priority to experience, to feelings, to emotions, to a "living through" of the effect of his decision upon himself and the members of his family, and to base his decision on these factors rather than on

logical argumentation or theoretical presuppositions.

Let me give another simple but significant example of this concern for the experiential. The use of simulation games is becoming more and more prevalent as a means of introducing new problems or issues. The intent of the game is to get the participant to simulate experiences surrounding a particular issue or problem. One of the purposes is to explicate the variety of options available not only in approaching the problem but in responding to it. The simulation game depends on a high degree of participation and communal interaction. The philosophy of such a game is to encourage one to feel or experience some aspect of reality about which he is concerned instead of simply reflecting on it cognitively within a certain predetermined structure. It might be argued that the simulation game is merely another more subtle way of getting one into a substitutionary experiential process and a technique for avoiding real decisions. That is, of course, the danger if one stops with only the simulation game. The intent of the process, however, is to highlight the importance not only of a person's formal learning but of his experiential background concerning any particular issue. One hopes that it also becomes, as some of my students call it, "a stimulation game" in which one is prodded to investigate the options experientially himself. But the theme exemplified in each of these illustrations is that experience should be not only the point of initiation but also the crucial norm in matters of judgment and decision. There is a significant and indispensable place, of course, for theoretical structures and careful reasoned reflection. However, those in the emerging culture insist that in their seeking a more meaningful life-style, priority rests with the experiential.

"If you haven't tried it, don't knock it," is a

colloquial way of expressing the priority of experience. The mind-set that this theme of the emerging culture seeks to reject is "the myth of objective consciousness." Objectivity is the paramount value of the technocracy. Personal experience cannot be the basis for reliable knowledge because it is too susceptible to human error, to corrupting influence of personal feelings, desires, and expectations. What is reliable knowledge upon which one can found his decisions about belief, valuation, and life-style?

The answer [for technocracy] is: reliable knowledge is knowledge that is scientifically sound, since science is that to which modern man refers for the definitive explication of reality. And what in turn is it that characterizes scientific knowledge? The answer is: objectivity. Scientific knowledge is not just feeling or speculation or subjective ruminating. It is a verifiable description of reality that exists independent of any purely personal considerations. It is true . . . real . . . dependable. . . . It works.[1]

We depend on experts in this mind-set in virtually every compartment of our lives because they have cultivated an objective consciousness. This is not easily acquired and takes intensive training by "the disciplining of attention and selected habits of thought, the screening out of other sources of consciousness, control over emotions, and a commitment to private and public honesty, to care and precision, to technical statement and social cooperation."[2] Roszak and Novak maintain that we create a myth, a special consciousness, a sense of reality, which we find necessary to inculcate through our educational institutions. We work feverishly to convince students that this is what constitutes reliable knowledge and that decisions about matters of importance, determination of values, significant actions, style of life, even belief in God must have justifiable reasons that can be articulated and are, at least theoretically, subject to public confirmation.

This objective consciousness is ultimately at the core, I think, of what Prof. Van A. Harvey, of the University of Pennsylvania, describes as "the morality of knowledge" which first found its expression in the eighteenth century, later was linked to the professional spheres of inquiry, and finally became educational policy for the university. It became incorporated in the scientific and technical mentality. One of its characteristic statements, cited by Harvey, is William K. Clifford's declaration that "it is wrong, everywhere, and for anyone, to believe anything on insufficient evidence."[3] The issue here is what really constitutes "sufficient evidence." For "morality of knowledge," technical reason is the final arbitrator.

This objective consciousness appeared sufficient and perhaps necessary for a child of the eighteenth century. The important question for the future of the culture is whether it is sufficient for a child of the twentieth century. This attitude has "dominated the consciousness of the Western intellectual" since the Enlightenment.[4] The emerging culture declares that it is just this consciousness which is being radically called into question and in fact needs to be transformed. The initial problem raised by this objective consciousness is that it appears to have too limited a view and appreciation of the human person. It leans toward a rationalistic conception of man that, in failing to attribute comparable worth to man's feelings, intuition, and nonintellective capacities, tends to diminish not only the experience but also the life of man himself. In this objective consciousness, man tends to assume the role of a computer into which he need only get all the proper information programmed and the direction of his life will be clear and secure even if it lacks vision and depth.

BELIEF AND THE COUNTER CULTURE

The primary characteristic of the computer is control. We think of speed, efficiency, and accuracy, but the overall organizing image is that of control. The computer can handle only data that has been properly programmed into it. In order for that programming to occur, the data must be processed, structured, and packaged. Our society has become obsessed by control, not only control of persons but, perhaps far more important, control of our experiences. We dread facing any situation with which we cannot cope. Goals of our society have been in terms of structure, organization, and implementation. It has become a questionable consequence of American pragmatism to measure human growth and maturity on the basis of one's capacity to cope with and to adapt to all situations. Whereas this is theoretically a laudable goal, in practicality, coping and adapting have come to be defined in terms of control and manipulation. We sift and filter our experience on the basis of certain limited presuppositions to make sure that nothing radically new ever happens. The greatest embarrassment of a technological man is to be authentically surprised or taken off guard by what confronts him. There is a kind of sterility, an artificiality about a perspective that causes man to guard the perimeters of his experience and to be suspicious of too sudden or extensive an expansion of his awareness or of his mind.

It is not really so astounding with this paradigm of controlled individuality that many within the dominant culture should be extraordinarily threatened when some of the young declare as a standing thesis that we should let it "all hang out." This involves exposing our own expectations, fears, desires, and doubts. However, we do not want anything to hang out that we are not in control of. A young man in one of my study seminars on "Belief and the Counter Culture" offered an eloquent testimony

to this apparently artificial stance when he declared, "If my dad would lose his cool only once, then I would believe he was for real!"

There are innumerable examples throughout our society of ways in which we attempt to control and manipulate our experience. We seek to avoid not only genuine surprise but also, of course, major change, which is always threatening. Let me give first a rather commonplace example simply because I think it is indicative of the kind of feeling response that extends throughout the dominant life-style. Imagine what happens when you prepare to take a vacation, particularly if it involves an aspect of camping. The object is to get everything prepared and organized before you leave. The food and equipment are organized, the pop-up trailer with a built-in tent is examined, the route is carefully planned, usually with the advice and assistance of a motor club or oil company, and all the places you intend to see are studied so you know what to expect before you get there. Then you carry through the meticulously planned vacation camping trip. The entire experience is controlled to make sure that nothing really new happens. At a given tourist attraction if you don't see something described in the glossy brochure, you ask the guide why you missed it. Then, finally, you wonder why the vacation was hectic, tiring, not really as exciting and different as expected. Yet you had worked very hard to see that it correlated with your expectations. Perhaps it is the repetition of just this kind of experience in one's youth that makes many of our young people today "hit the road" with no plans about where they are headed. At least here the originality, beauty, and even contradictory character of the experiences that confront them will not be minimized or smothered. The zeal to experience life more fully does not protect young people from potential failure or even tragedy. But this same spirit cries out against squandering their lives in "packaged plans." Perhaps the best example of controlled experience comes in the educational process. In the study seminars I conducted on the counter culture, it was precisely in the area of education that the greatest sense of resentment and rebellion was expressed. This was not only by the young, but by their elders as well. One of the young men in a study seminar was identifying himself to the group and he said that he attended a regional high school where he learned all day—then he immediately corrected himself and said, "No, where I'm taught all day." If one understands education as that which enables him to engage creatively and fulfillingly with his environment and culture as a natural and essential part of the human condition, then it appears that often school has more to do with technical training and role socialization then it does with creative engagement. The emphasis within too many of our schools is on the acquisition of information, opinions, and processes which, when regurgitated in certain set patterns, brings maximum approval and reward by the system. As Reich suggests, the school system often appears most interested in training students to stop thinking and to start obeying.[5] The educational process appears to be preparing people to fulfill certain necessary roles within the society. When we say that a student had an outstanding academic career, we often mean that he went through a process evaluated by standard means of testing that indicated he would be functionally successful and therefore useful to the system. The ironic thing is that even this assumption apparently is not valid. Recent studies have indicated that there seems to be no significant correlation between an outstanding academic record and success in a profession.[6]

In a very provocative and stimulating film entitled *Why Man Creates*, there is a symbolic sequence about the manufacture of Ping-Pong balls.[7] One ball goes beyond the established requirements of the others by bouncing far too high. When this extraordinary behavior is observed, bells ring and sirens wail. The discordant Ping-Pong ball is immediately shunted out of the process and rejected by the system. This is probably analogous to what happens in the system to one who attempts to expand and experiment too radically with his experience. If one does not adapt to the controlled standards of the system, he is ostracized or rejected.

It is my suspicion that much of recent campus unrest really has at its foundation a radical despair and skepticism about the presuppositions and styles of contemporary education. The emerging culture is declaring that this theme of the priority of experience must find an authentic expression within the educational process. This would, of course, require a transformation of consciousness or a revision of one's expectations about what education involves. There is an attempt to recover the humanity ironically absent in Hodgell's caricature of *The Professor*.

In high school, college, and graduate levels, new models are beginning to emerge that insist on taking seriously not only the formal education of students and teachers alike but also their experience. Instead of having a set format, the class becomes a contractual arrangement where all the participants through a dialogue determine the most fruitful options for focusing on a particular issue or problem. In other words, the members of the class or seminar determine their own priorities which arise out of their natural interests and curiosity and their own human experience. The process itself is authentically communal. This does not mean that the students simply subdivide a topic or responsibility for the purposes of research and then sew together

THE PROFESSOR

This print is available from Robert Hodgell, Box 46813, Pass-a-Grille Beach, Florida 33741

(often ineptly) their independent conclusions. Rather, the entire class becomes an experiential and dialogical situation in which students and teachers alike stimulate, correct, reorient, and revise work as it is in process. Theses or conclusions are presented by various class teams not only in verbal presentations but by employing a multiplicity of media. This might involve using simulation games, films, sound experiences, and art objects, to name but a few. The research project is then revised on the basis of the suggestions and criticisms of the group as a whole. Finally, the objective testing or evaluative process by the teacher alone, which has often been a means to compel implicit conformity, has been rejected in favor of self-evaluation. The members of the group scrutinize their own work and present not only an evaluation of it but the criteria upon which that evaluation was reached. This evaluation is concerned not primarily with how much factual data was accumulated but with the contribution of the total experience to one's life-style, sensitivity, and growth as an individual. The fundamental criterion for this experience is the degree to which this educational process might be considered humanizing.

The dominant educational process for all grade and graduate levels, at least in its present form, not only is characterized by the control of experience but also is one of the major factors in creating or fashioning a consciousness that many judge to be false or at least not very humane. Therefore, many young see the educational system as something from which one drops out, or perhaps in a more active sense now, something that is actually to be resisted. Many of those who have been drawn into this cultural revolution have consciously set out to widen their experience and expand their awareness and sensitivity. This means first simply living through more and different kinds of events.

In growing numbers the young are actively rejecting what has been described as stable and guided forms of education and mature development. They are predisposed to de-emphasize formal education and stress the variety and quality of one's experiential encounters. This means for many simply dropping out of formal education and taking to the road. This motif was foreshadowed in the early experience of one of the bards of the emerging culture—one might even say philosophers—Bob Dylan. He found a rather brief stay at the University of Minnesota to be less educational than "knocking around" the country encountering the diversity and plurality of human personalities and situations. These experiences formed the foundation for the insights and assertions that emerge in his music and his hauntingly persuasive lyrics. Although Dylan's present life is not characterized as being "on the road," this earlier wandering was surely a component in his growth as an artist and as a person. Many youth find this model to be attractive and an example of almost the only way to introduce into their education an aspect that is authentically free and experiential. There is also the refusal of many to accept a permanent vocational decision. Therefore, an individual commits himself to a particular job only as long as it is meaningful and contributes to his own personal growth in terms of the expansion of awareness as well as to the growth of the community with which he is engaged. This does not mean that one abdicates social responsibility, but it does mean that he refuses to let himself be *possessed* by his vocation.

There is a strong feeling of alienation from the role of the expert. A professional career involving long and arduous preparation for a highly specialized and skilled service is no longer so attractive. The judgment is that often, although not necessarily, professional training tends to narrow a person's sensitivities and places an inappropriate value on the accumulation of rather limited and highly technical knowledge or skill. The emerging culture will be characterized by an even higher degree of mobility than we know presently. If this vocational freedom is pursued neither whimsically nor as escapism, then this new mobility may provide a whole new context in which creative experiences and opportunities are realized. The presuppositions of society cannot be allowed to prescribe or limit one's human options. The assertion is that one must attempt to be exposed to a wide spectrum of options by any practicable means available. He must then investigate these options with energy and enthusiasm.

Poster art of the counter culture often satirizes the aspirations of the dominant society, particularly those actions which seek to control or manipulate one's experience, consciousness, or attitude. This can be done in a form that appears blatantly banal or even profane by utilizing the traditionally revered symbols of the established society to make a critique. Therefore, the posters often have a second level of satire in the various "camp" forms employed.

One of the manifestations of the attempt to control experience and, therefore, at least implicitly dictate societal goals has been the process of certification. In most schools the extent to which a student fulfills or adapts to academic demands determines relatively early how far he moves up the educational ladder. This in turn determines who has the opportunity to gain status, greater economic rewards, or social mobility. It has become a satiric joke that now one needs a master's degree or even a doctorate to be a ditchdigger. What this implies, of course, is that the university is the focal point for the testing and certification game. One might also suggest that the university often produces certification in areas that have very little if anything to do with the actual function one will perform in a given profession or occupation. Therefore, some in the emerging culture are encouraging the university to get out of the certification business. As Harvey Cox, of Harvard, suggested recently in an address, what we need is to create a "fantasy university."[8] The business of certification could be left to the particular profession as it already is via bar, medical, and ordination examinations. Since businesses increasingly provide on-the-job training for their men, they ought also to certify them for specific positions, if there is any need for certification at all. This would leave the university in a position to pursue an educational goal of seeking the truth or at least seeking new insights in diverse fields. The university would then become a resource center of personnel, research material, and books. One could presuppose that every member of a particular class seminar or lab was authentically interested in the subject matter and was questing after some inspiration or clarification in this regard. It would allow us to encourage what Cox has called, "intellectual orgies." Here a student or teacher would be able to follow out his interest and natural curiosity about a given topic without always having to stop and begin another project in order to develop the proper balance as decreed by those who administer the educational system. It is my judgment that this kind of educational process would first create a much smaller and perhaps a more genuinely educational institution than our present academic gargantua. Also, such a process would probably produce, or at least allow, more creative leaps of the imagination, better integration of experience and theory, and might also generate a kind of excitement and stimulation that would make the university a place where one could

WAR IS GOOD BUSINESS

more consistently develop his natural interest and unique talents.

A more far-reaching position is assumed by the social critic Paul Goodman, who suggests that education ought to take as its model the way in which speech is learned by a young child.[9] The emphasis here is on "incidental education." This means that education is best developed by example and by participatory involvement in the ongoing activities of a given society. It is in this rather natural and instinctive process that teaching and learning best occur. He contends, among other things, that most high schools should be eliminated in favor of other kinds of youth communities that are more conducive to education. Also, so-called higher education at the college and at the university and graduate-school levels should be taken up after one enters a profession and not before. If his judgments about the educational process are correct and his suggestions therapeutic, these are moves which society is likely to make only quite gradually, if at all. A thorough transformation of consciousness in reference to education will be required if that revision is to occur.

At the root of what the counter culture believes to be a deficient technocratic consciousness is the idea that man makes his ethical decisions according to principles that have a rational undergirding and for which he can give evidence. However, we are becoming more and more aware that argumentation has very little to do with actual performance. Rather, Novak notes, "As the novelist well knows, men act chiefly under the psychic pressure of symbols, of images, of models; words, principles, and rationalizations come much later."[10] Those formative symbols and images are more a creation of man's "nonintellective" capacities than of his reason. The power and significance of symbols will occupy us in Chapter V. The point here is that a transformation of consciousness would reflect a more wholistic understanding of man. This understanding requires that the authentic priority of experience and of subjective involvement be recognized and allowed to function in shaping the culture of a people.

A radical subjectivity has come to characterize the emerging culture. The efforts to expand one's awareness and sensitivity have had as their goal the recovery of an authentic self. The emerging culture has a preoccupation with the self as a starting point. No doubt this is partially a reaction to what is understood as the principal threat of technocracy, namely the pervasive extension of techniques that results in the sterile and oppressive manipulation of one's experience and life-style. Technology itself is not condemned out of hand by the emerging culture, since even technology has potentialities for humanization. What this culture rejects is such an extensive and pervasive use of techniques that there is a leveling, compartmentalizing, and categorizing of human experience that leads to a process of dehumanization.

This concern for radical subjectivity is an attempt to liberate the self from controlled experience and imposed consciousness. The emphasis has been on an individual's sorting out of his own priorities and then acting upon them. This has fostered such expressions as "do your own thing" or "get your thing together." This is not intended to encourage an ego trip where all final evaluation is focused on subjective whims or where another person's authenticity is jeopardized. Quite to the contrary, there is an attempt to identify genuine priorities of the self which are founded on the basis of the intrinsic worth of each human being—a human being who becomes full and fulfilled precisely in community with others.

This theme is dramatically illustrated by Frederick Perls. His statement, in its full context, has become a kind of motto for some elements of the counter culture:

I do my thing, and you do your thing.
I am not in this world to live up to your expectations
And you are not in this world to live up to mine.
You are you and I am I,
And if by chance we find each other,
It's beautiful.[11]

This radical subjectivity is founded not only on the basis of intrinsic human authenticity and integrity but also on the basis of significant involvement both with other persons and with the environment. Discovering one's priorities demands personal involvement.

Many young people are declaring that it is not the exclusion of the personal that makes knowledge reliable, that is, meaningful, but precisely the opposite is the case. Truth is subjectivity. This theme is being heard more and more frequently in the counter culture. It is frequently interpreted as being antirational or anti-intellectual. The new emerging culture is condemned for disparaging reason and failing to appreciate the crucial contributions of disciplined, reasoned reflection. Yet the principal thrust of the critique made by the counter culture is not antirational; it is instead antirationalistic. "The accusations [of the counter culture] are not attacks upon intelligence, accurate understanding, or good judgment but upon the myth of objectivity as too narrow an expression of reason, which leaves out of consideration too many delicate but crucial operations of human intelligence."[12] This form of radical subjectivity which is akin to that of the Danish philosopher Søren Kierkegaard does not mean that there are no criteria for truth or falsity, right or wrong, depth or shallowness,

but that these cannot be apprehended within the sphere of neutral objective analysis.[13] It might be argued that it is rather the technological man in his preoccupation with objective consciousness who really fails to appreciate the full capacity of reason and therefore is truly antirational.

Objective consciousness may be the ideal for the technician, yet it is in striking contrast to the philosophy of science espoused by some rather prominent scientists. Michael Polanyi has produced a most penetrating study of the personal role of the knower in science in his work *Personal Knowledge*.[14] He rejects the absolute dichotomy between objectivity in science and subjectivity in areas such as religion and ethics. He maintains that the scientist exercises personal judgment in the evaluation of evidence and in the selection of a given model or theory to guide further research. In a recent article, Polanyi has asserted further the subjective involvement of the scientist in what he calls the "dynamics of tacit knowing" which is kept moving by the combination of imagination and intuition, "imagination-*cum*-intuition."[15] Intuition and imagination, like experience, have become for the counter culture precious, almost sacred. Reason has become identified in the counter culture with a kind of sterile, calculating, and manipulative force. It distances itself from a person, object, or experience in order to control it. Reason has come to be seen not as that which liberates or illumines what it encounters, but rather something that imprisons its object. The rationalistic tendencies of the dominant society have associated reflection with controlling reason. Reason has lost its soul, it has been cut off from the self or the personal element that gave it vigor, flexibility, and openness. Reason has become rationalistic and therefore antihuman.

The counter culture is not antirational but rather suggests that we need to develop a broader concept of reason than is presently accepted in technocracy—a concept of reason that is more humane, personal, and intuitive. This is a kind of ecstatic or foundational reason that is characterized by its receptive nature and its experiential quality. If this cultural revolution is to effect a change of consciousness, it must emphasize a kind of reflection or thinking that is not based on man's objectively disposing of the subject matter from a position of distance, but rather that grows out of an occurrence or event which happens to him. This is a kind of receiving reason that is wholistic and therefore humane. It is not cut off from its sources but is placed within the context of a human being struggling for clarity as well as insight. We are seeking a reformation of our understanding of reason that rejects technical or calculative thought as an inadequate form of reflection. We are searching for a form of reason that finds a place for the intuitive leaps of the imagination and for receptive encounters with other objects, experiences, or persons. Such reasoning is not establishing facts from a distance but, rather, involves experience and encounter. Illumination, vision, may occur via the function of a type of reason that includes the nonintellective capacities of man. This reason may allow man to discover symbols that are determinative for the fulfillment of human potential, are able to expand his capacity to experience. Perhaps most important, such reason may facilitate more satisfying and creative transactions with one's fellowmen and a transcendent reality that many call God.

Radical subjectivity depends, however, on involvement. No one may dictate another's priorities, but, on the other hand, neither can they be worked out in abstraction or in isolation. Open, creative, and dialogical encounter with other persons and with one's culture is imperative. A selfless and soulless reason dependent on controlled and limited experience results in dehumanized, sterile, and joyless life. These characteristic motifs of the emerging culture—priority of experience and subjective involvement—are based on a profound appreciation of persons. The intrinsic human worth of every human being emphasizes the cruciality of expanded awareness and heightened sensitivities. This necessitates involvement with and commitment to others which implies a continual expansion of one's experience. This attitude also rejects a constitutional distrust and suspicion of everyone else and every new experience which has become so characteristic of our time. Subjective involvement (radical subjectivity) fosters a new trust between persons. It encourages one to risk his ideas, his position, and even himself for the sake of a new and more fulfilling experience and relationship with another. This new understanding of reason allows the mind to be liberated so as not to dominate experience but rather to be subject to experience. It frees one in this expanding experience to reach out and touch and embrace another not only physically but with his mind and feelings as well. This produces among those who participate in the new emerging culture a sense of mystery about human experience. It entices them toward bursts of creativity that culminate in moments of awe or mystery. The aim is not to contain and control this mystery but rather to appreciate it and celebrate it. The vision of the humane calls us to fling open the doors that imprison our experience and let our spirit fly free.

NOTES

1. Theodore Roszak, *The Making of a Counter Culture* (Anchor Book, Doubleday & Company, Inc., 1969), p. 208.
2. Michael Novak, *The Experience of Nothingness* (Harper & Row, Publishers, Inc., 1970), p. 37.

3. Van A. Harvey, "The Alienated Theologian," in Robert A. Evans (ed.), *The Future of Philosophical Theology* (The Westminster Press, 1971), p. 119.

4. *Ibid.*, p. 118.

5. Charles A. Reich, *The Greening of America* (Random House, Inc., 1970) p. 131.

6. "Donald Hoyt, for American College Testing, 1965, found that college grades have no correlation with life achievement in any profession." (Paul Goodman, *The New Reformation* [Random House, Inc., 1970], p. 72.)

7. Kaiser Aluminum and Chemical Corporation, *Why Man Creates*, distributed by Pyramid Films, Santa Monica, California.

8. Harvey Cox, presented on a taped address on "The Role of the University," prepared for *Symposium 70*, Learning, Inc., Hamden, Conn.

9. Goodman, *New Reformation*, p. 69.

10. Michael Novak (ed.), *American Philosophy in the Future* (Charles Scribner's Sons, 1968), p. 10.

11. This phrase by Perls appears frequently in the poster art of the counter culture. I have been unable to locate the original source.

12. Novak, *Nothingness*, p. 36.

13. D. Z. Phillips, "Subjectivity and Religious Truth in Kierkegaard," in Jerry H. Gill (ed.), *Philosophy Today*, No. 2, (London: Macmillan & Co., Ltd., 1969), p. 113.

14. Michael Polanyi, *Personal Knowledge: Towards a Post-Critical Philosophy* (The University of Chicago Press, 1959).

15. Michael Polanyi, "Sense-Giving and Sense-Reading," in Gill (ed.), *Philosophy Today*, No. 2, p. 306.

IV

Mystery and Creativity

One day in late fall a train was slowly winding through the mountainous area of Kentucky. A journalist found himself sitting next to a young man who seemed exceedingly nervous. As they rode along they fell into conversation, and the young man began to share some experiences that accounted for his tension. He was going home after serving a two-year term in the federal penitentiary for resisting the draft.

Three years before he had been the pride of a small town in Kentucky. He was an outstanding student, president of his senior class, and had received several football scholarships to universities in the area. During his first year at college, as a result of rethinking his own priorities, there were radical changes in his understanding of himself. He decided to participate only in amateur athletics, since he found university intervarsity sports to be so competitive and commercial that they were dehumanizing. Perhaps more important, he decided to refuse induction into the military service, because he had reached the judgment that the Vietnam war was both immoral and inhuman.

The subsequent trial in the county seat brought confusion, anxiety, and embarrassment not only to his family but to the entire community, who failed to understand the reasons for this change.

The widespread publicity and controversy caused his parents to be ostracized and isolated within the community. He was unable to explain his motivations and actions to his parents, and the possibility for any real communication between them was severed.

During the time he was in prison his parents neither visited nor wrote him, nor did he initiate correspondence with them. However, a few days before he was released a friend was visiting him and he asked the friend to take a message to his parents. The young man asked his friend to explain to his family that he was getting out of prison and that he wanted to come home. However, he knew that he had disgraced the family in the eyes of the community, and he did not want to hurt them further, so he had worked out a plan. He would be arriving by train, and just outside the town there was a big oak tree near the track. If they wanted him to come home, they were to tie a ribbon on the lower branch of the tree and he would know that it was all right to return to them. However, if the ribbon was not on the tree, he would stay on the train and ride right on through. As they approached the town the young man became more and more nervous. He explained that he was afraid to look and asked the journalist to watch for him. The familiar hills about the village flicked by the window of the train. As they rounded the final turn, the reporter shouted: "Hey! Look!" The young man glanced up and saw that the entire tree was covered with ribbons.

Tears sprang to the young man's eyes and he was overcome by a sense of mystery, wonder, and joy. This testimony of love and acceptance by his parents was really beyond comprehension and certainly beyond explanation. There was a hidden depth to their action that defied analysis and invoked a sense of overwhelming awe. He had not really been separated from the love of his parents by a different understanding and commitment. In that instant the anxiety and pain of separation was erased. A bridge toward real communication was begun. And this had been built creatively and joyously.

This simple, joyous expression of love may be a parable for the second theme of the emerging culture—a recovery of mystery and a restoration of creativity. To exert a humanizing influence is one of the primary concerns of the cultural revolution. This concern may be in reaction to what many within the counter culture believe to be the stifling and dehumanizing effects of a technocratic and bureaucratic society.

The criteria for what it means to be human or even the model for this new humanity are far from clear. However, intuitive appreciation of the mysterious with a stress on the free expression of one's feelings, particularly joy, which results in the restoration of creativity, is at the heart of the vision of the human. I hope the "joy kick" will be with us for some time to come. But for joy really to have a "kick," for it to have a significant impact that transforms one's consciousness and life-style, it must be more than the superficial "celebration of celebration."

On what basis is the emerging culture joyous and celebrative? What enables one to risk himself and express his feelings? What liberates one to be creative and experimental without an immediate application for the creative act in view? The answers may lie in a recovery of the human and particularly in an appreciation and recovery of mystery. So much of our everyday experience within technological society has become routinized and compartmentalized that we automatically accept classification by social security numbers and IBM cards, and our activities are subconsciously pigeonholed. Roles and expectations for housewives, professionals, and students seem so determined that we could almost list the principal activities we will be engaged in two years from now. The patterns are so set we often feel internally "programmed" by our present consciousness. In rebellion against this obsession for control and categorization the emerging culture has initiated a creative search for that which produces wonder and awe. The young have sought mystical experiences in order to find an alternative to the calculation, measuring, and manipulation of the established culture.

As Lewis Mumford suggests, everything has been routinized until it functions like clockwork.[1] The clock is the "paragon of automatons" and automation is the key to the systems. So the young satirize the control of time by establishing communes that reject the significance of the system's time. However, this restless attitude is not confined to life in communes. Those who are more timid, and still imprisoned by time instead of freed from it, symbolize their rebellion by having big bright watches adorned by the countenance of Mickey Mouse or Spiro Agnew. The desire is not only for physical freedom but also for mental and spiritual liberation. One's future should be open to new possibilities that hold the promise of significant and meaningful human activities.

This quest for the mystical which often characterizes the counter culture is, I believe, a yearning for a new sense of meaning and freedom which is authentic. These "neomystics" are on a quest for the holy and perhaps for God. This quest is inseparable from their search for the human and is tied up with their search for an "authentically human style of life."[2]

The concern with the mystical ought not to be seen, I think, as either an escapist or an isolationist position. The search for the mystical has been primarily in a direction that would heighten one's sensibility and allow for recovery of the self. This recovery of the self is not for its own sake but rather a way to liberate one for more significant involvement with others. There are, however, sizable inhibitions in this kind of personal encounter. William Stringfellow offers this perceptive analysis of contemporary dancing:

Even popular dancing avoids involvement with others nowadays and becomes a solitary exercise with many characteristics of a fantasy experience in which you twist and contort and burlesque your body but never touch or hold or embrace your partner and, in fact, just dance alone, as if beguiled with the thought of involvement but still afraid to become involved.[3]

There is an attraction-repulsion syndrome operative here because a significant encounter involves exposure and subjects one to a threat against his own personhood. This seems particularly true in reference to the expression of feelings and emotions. If you ask someone how he *feels* about a particular experience or person, he is quite likely to begin to explain in some detail what he *thinks* about the experience. There is almost an automatic substitution of the cognitive for the emotive. Our highly complex and technical society has taught us rather well how to control or mask our emotions. We have been instructed by the dominant society that it is somehow inappropriate to express one's feelings honestly and directly to another. This includes feelings of grief, anger, joy, and love. Granger Westberg makes this point very perceptively in regard to grief when he notes how difficult it is for a man, particularly in our society, to cry. Westberg has an excellent illustration of this:

When a little boy falls and skins his knee and cries out in fright and pain, someone picks him up and says, "Now, now, little man, don't cry." And when he is eight years old and hurts himself, he does not dare to cry, nor at eighteen when something happens about which he ought to cry. At thirty-eight when some great loss is suffered, he *cannot* cry.[4]

We have in our society not only a conspiracy against grief but against the free expression of almost any human emotion.

This restraint is equally applicable to anger. The conditions of our society have urged us to muffle our expressions of hostility and strong disagreement. This is true not only with strangers and casual acquaintances but it is also true among friends and even family members. Families often attempt to keep things cool and calm by avoiding controversy and argumentation altogether. Or if it emerges, the tendency is to keep it on a very issue-oriented level. Expression of personal anger, hostility, and certainly hate are prohibited. So although one may be screaming inside about a personal hurt or concern, the voice is to be kept cool and the issue abstract. What often results is that the emotion is not adequately dealt with, and is only suppressed until, like a ball pushed underwater, it pops up at another point. Therefore, the hostility may take another and even more insidious form.

Because these feelings are not adequately dealt with as they arise, neither the person nor the one he is encountering accepts himself or another as a complete human being capable of a wide range of emotional expression. Our relationships with others are compartmentalized into socially acceptable patterns. Therefore, we develop masks of control because we are afraid to deal with the full range of our own or another's humanity.

However, for the emerging culture, one other area of the expression of one's feelings is perhaps even more tragic. We seem unable to crack our rigidity long enough to express enthusiastically our joy, love, or appreciation.

This poster about the need to be told you are loved expresses eloquently what every counselor knows from experience. Most people are unable to find adequate ways of communicating their affection and concern with one another as persons and not as objects.

Life has become so mechanical and sterile that it is characterized by a kind of joylessness. Thus the counter culture is trying to revive a liberated manifestation of joy simply in the awareness of being alive. Ultimately, joy threatens control more than any other human emotion. Therefore, the counter culture has relished what I call the "joy kick." Joy involves not only the emotions but also the whole body. There is a hang-up in our society about touching one another. Touching a person, except for the formalized gesture of a handshake, for instance, is a violation of the person's privacy and individuality, but it also expresses a sense of commitment and engagement with another. Vacillation between adhering to social mores and genuinely expressing one's feelings is satirized in what has been described to me as the "Oklahoma hug." This is an embrace where you draw a person to you with one arm but hold him away with the other. We seem caught between a desire for involvement, acceptance, and commitment, and, on the other hand, a reluctance to risk ourselves in order to reap the joy of this kind of human encounter.

The reluctance to embrace physically is only the final manifestation of our reluctance to embrace mentally and emotionally. To express feelings freely or to become involved with another without taking that person or the context in which he operates seriously is, of course, a violation of the integrity of the relationship. But before one can risk himself, before he can emotionally and physically embrace and commit himself to another, he must in some sense know who he is, he must recover the self. The involvement with mysticism and particularly contemplation appears to many in the emerging culture important for this revitalization of one's self.

Though the hungry exploration for peace, both in the world and within one's self, may provoke frantic activity, it can also lead to contemplation. Contemplation is a discipline to aid in achieving a particular state of consciousness. It is an attempt to be still, open, and receptive to that transcendent reality which undergirds our human existence and which reveals itself in such a manner as to fashion or guide our way of life. It is intended to supplement and facilitate human involvement and commitment, not to substitute for it. Harvey Cox suggests that there is a striking resemblance between contemplation and festivity because they both free one from the normal preoccupation with routine for an immediate experience of "joy, appreciation, and anticipation."[5]

Often those who meditate and those who celebrate claim that drugs or liquor help. You can choose your side of the culture gap on that question. There is great ambiguity in arguments about whether one's using marijuana and what have come to be called the psychedelic drugs means turning on or copping out. Nevertheless, it is certain that this will be an important topic not only for discussion but probably more important for continued research and investigation. In this work I have sought quite consciously to de-emphasize, if not to defuse, the explosive preoc-

NOT ONLY TO BE LOVED BUT·TO·BE·TOLD·THAT·I·AM·LOVED THE REALM OF SILENCE IS LARGE ENOUGH BEYOND THE GRAVE

SILENCE

cupation with the use of drugs in relationship to the counter culture. It is a topic, I have discovered from my study seminars, upon which both young and old are extraordinarily volatile, but not very cogent. However, significant clarification can occur on the basis of more intensive study and discussion which are sometimes stimulated by the seminar.

The use of the so-called "soft" drugs is an area where preconceptions and prejudices are rampant. There is simply a need for considerable more data derived from careful research on this matter than we presently possess in order to make any careful judgments. The subject demands investigation from a variety of perspectives ranging from the historical experimentation of William James with nitrous oxide to the reflections of some contemporary theologians such as Frederick Ferré about whether the controlled use of drugs will aid or induce a mystical experience. The potential and dangers of this phenomenon are yet to be fully examined. The histrionics about the subject greatly inhibit that research.

My reason for minimizing the drug culture debate is that this discussion itself can become a primary form of copping out. The more significant and perhaps prevelant question is not whether the use of soft drugs (marijuana, psychedelics) is dangerous or therapeutic, for this has more to do with the use versus the abuse of drugs, which has not to date been clearly distinguished. Rather, the more important question concerns what drug use says about a person's present consciousness or what he hopes it will become. The real issue involves why people experiment either with drugs or alcohol. Does one anticipate an expansion of the mind and therefore heightened awareness, or is it an attempt to escape to another world than that which confronts one? Does it allow one to find release at least momentarily from an imposed consciousness and life-style, or is it an attempt to create a more artificial yet fulfilling and satisfying environment? Does it enhance one's capacity to communicate and encounter another person or community? Or does it tend to isolate one further from an authentic relationship to himself as well as to others? What we are desperately in need of is not simply additional data but some criteria by which we can evaluate the benefits and liabilities of consuming intoxicating substances. We must begin to ask whether it contributes to the humane. Does it enhance or detract from the possibility of expanding one's awareness, appreciating the mysterious, restoring creativity, facilitating communication, enabling communiality, or making one more open to the graciousness of the transcendent? These are the kinds of questions around which our research and reflection must focus.

The question of criteria for the humane, particularly in regard to drugs, must be faced by the emerging culture. The contradictions evident in the counter culture are betrayed even by its language. What could be more technological than "turned on," "tuned in," or "vibes"? Why aren't the metaphors from nature rather than from electronic circuitry? The parentage is clear. Today's young people are "children of the technocracy." To "turn on" via manipulation, via drugs, is the epitome of the plastic world. The children of the technocracy are struggling to become parents of a new culture. The irony obvious in one's seeking "freedom" through manipulation can and is being pondered, but total, indiscriminate, and suppressive reactions by the dominant society to the mere mention of drugs do not facilitate this resolution.

The use of drugs must be put in some kind of perspective. It may not be coincidental that the emergence of the counter culture parallels the rise in drug use in this country; this is surely a facet of reaching out and seeking new experience. However, this relationship has been sensationalized to the degree that for many the image of the emerging culture has been inextricably bound to the drug culture. Let me stress again my conviction that this is a superficial identification, but this must not be a means of sidesteping an important issue. It should be reiterated that the employment of intoxicating substances is hardly a unique phenomenon of our culture.[6] A wide variety of elements intended to facilitate contemplation or celebration have been employed almost from the outset of recorded history. To draw the question of abuse into perspective, recorded data indicates that the incidence of alcoholism in America is many times greater than instances of drug addiction. Due to the fact that alcoholism is more extensive, the toll in human sensibilities as well as material resources is probably greater in reference to alcohol. It is perfectly clear that addiction to "hard" drugs (heroin, morphine) is as debilitating and destructive as severe alcoholism, and I am not seeking to minimize the tragedy of either. Both epitomize the unnatural and the manipulative, since both rob one of genuine freedom and openness to the future. However, it seems somewhat disproportionate to consider one an illness and the other a crime.[7] It seems to me to be premature to condemn categorically the use of either marijuana or psychedelics, although that condemnation would be applicable to the abuse of either substance. We are not presently in a position to give a definitive answer about the detriments or the benefits of either substance even in moderation. Prohibition in either case does not seem feasible. What we need to do is to engage each other across the culture gap in substantive and sustained conversations about the use of any intoxicating substance in relationship to what it

means to be human. Many persons who associate themselves with the motifs and themes of the emerging culture are trying to get precisely at the issue of what contributes to the human. In this process they are encouraging others to set aside or even pass beyond the stage of experimenting with drugs in order to get at the more crucial and fundamental issues. There is a sense in which the drive to get to more natural and personal forms of illumination is becoming predominant. It appears that the use of intoxicating substances ultimately represses rather than liberates the spirit.

The fascination and the fear of drugs characteristic of the dominant culture sometimes get transferred to the ecstatic or mystical experience as well. Here, too, fascination and fear intermingle. First, there is already a recognition, particularly in religious circles, of the "erosion of mystery." But there is also a fear not only of the neomystics (since the church has always been unsettled by the mystics) but fear of mystery itself, which seems vague, incomprehensible, and most threatening, uncontrollable. This uneasiness is manifested not only by a suspicion of the spiraling interest in mystical traditions such as Zen Buddhism but also in an essential distrust of groups speaking in tongues or the so-called Jesus freaks. These mystically oriented groups simply do not fit readily within the categories of the religious establishment. Yet at the same time there is a need within the established religious tradition for a recovery of the sense of mystery and for a more wholistic understanding of man. Mystery points beyond a given event or act, such as the loving and reconciling gesture of the parents in the earlier story, to an undergirding and gracious power or reality. Mystery suggests that it is *possible* to encounter that ultimate reality. All is not determined, the future has not been foreclosed. Mystery holds the promise of a genuinely open future and of a gracious, transcendent, and sustaining reality that make life more humane. It is more humane because it offers authentic human transformation and renewal as not only a hope but a real possibility.

The counter culture has spawned various groups of neomystics who invest a major portion of their time in contemplation and the quest for the mysterious. However, it is important to recognize the significance of the recovery of mystery even apart from participation in a "mystic cult." Theologians such as Reinhold Niebuhr and Karl Rahner, not considered mystics, both claim that a sense of mystery is essential to man. For instance, Karl Rahner, one of the most prominent and distinguished Roman Catholic theologians, asserts that real humanity is impossible without this sense of mystery.[8] Rahner's emphasis on the intuitional aspects of man tend to keep experience and mystery in constant interaction. This highlights the role of the Holy Spirit in human experience. The new concern for the mystical seems to lead not toward a secular theology but rather toward a spiritual theology as the sign of the future. Thus members of churches and synagogues are delighted that the emerging culture appears to be more religious and deeply concerned because they often reject the institutional representatives of the major traditions.

The recovery of mystery appears destined to provide a guide for culture to broaden its sensitivities and also to be a guide for religious institutions. The church or synagogue is being forced to assess its own priorities and practices to see whether instead of being a place where mystery and awe are preserved, cherished, and proclaimed, it is the place where the mysterious has been eroded and awe-producing experiences suppressed for the sake of organizational efficiency and so-called relevance.

In the emerging culture, mystery is united with wonder. A recovery of the appreciation of the mysterious has heightened the sense of wonder. Many aspects of our human experience which had been considered prosaic if not unimportant have attained a new prominence. The flowering plant or a change of seasons has suddenly stimulated a whole new generation of people both young and old. There is an unprecedented migration on weekends to the forest preserves and wilderness areas.

A whole new generation of ecology buffs is crying out against an increasing assault on the environment by industry, corporate bodies, and individuals who pollute the air, the water, and the earth. The impetus for this protest comes not only from the threat to health, but, equally important, from a renewed attraction to the natural and the primitive simply because one has discovered here a new sense of joy and wonder. There does not appear to be an intensification of a kind of analytic and biological examination of the natural processes, but rather a direct appreciation and simple enjoyment of the natural processes.

The types of activities that are increasingly being engaged in are important here. One lies on his back in quietude and gazes into the trees and into the sky. One independently explores a wilderness area rather than following a marked nature trail where all the plants and trees are identified by little signs in their Latin names. One struggles through the winter woods on snowshoes, resting occasionally beside a tree to watch the wildlife. One also struggles to ban snowmobiles from the woods altogether, because of their disruptive noise and the destruction of the fauna. Many prefer cross-country skiing to slicing down neatly carved man-made trails after riding up in a mechanized lift.

We seem to be seeking here the classical mystical theme of "unmediated directness." A thirst for the taste of the holy grows as these encounters mirror and reveal the transcendent, mysterious, and wondrous. There is an attempt not to fragment and break up experiences by undue analysis and classification, organizing them into set categories. We launch an intensive quest for an encounter with that which points beyond itself and lifts us above ourselves in wonder and transformation.

However, this quest is not limited to the world of nature. A new appreciation for the miracle of human birth makes this an event which more parents want to experience directly and communally. The renewed emphasis on natural childbirth allows the wonder not only to be anticipated but to be cherished. Interest increases for making this a communal event so that not only the mother may share in the joy of the moment, but also the father. Such paternal interest sometimes erupts publicly in disputes with hospitals when a husband insists on being present in the labor and delivery room. In more isolated instances there is a return to childbirth within the home itself in the midst of a community.

We have a revival of appreciation for personal friendship where good "rap" sessions in terms of honest and penetrating conversations are the most important things occurring. During a visit to a college campus recently as a guest lecturer, I inquired of numerous students what the most important and exciting thing on campus was. The response was not in terms of studies, campus issues, political involvement, or even major social or athletic events, but rather simply good "raps" in small groups.

A revival of interest flourishes in the aesthetic mediums, particularly the graphic arts, dance, and, of course, music. This resurgence of interest in the aesthetic supports my suggestion in Chapter I of a "new Renaissance." However, a different emphasis does not lead simply to a search for Bach and Byron. A more important emphasis is your involvement and participation in the aesthetic and creative act. It is much more important to paint or to write your own poetry than to be a knowledgeable connoisseur of either area. Painting and poetry are not only shared communally but in fact are created communally.

We have in the merger of mystery and wonder a manifestation of some of the primary themes of the emerging culture. We have the mystical theme of unmediated direct encounter and involvement with the object, experience, or person in a subjective way, a communal fashioning and sharing of an experience, and a focus on creativity for its own sake.

It is the latter of these themes, the restoration of creativity, which is one of the dominant and crucial motifs of the emerging culture. The need to liberate the human spirit to be authentically original and creative is one of the major reasons why we need a transformation of consciousness.

To get one's emotive responses as well as his reflections attuned to the subject of creativity, I recommend the film cited in Chapter III, *Why Man Creates*. This film unfolds a myriad of colorful and probing images asking what is at the root of man's creative capacity. The film seems to proclaim, although it does not pontificate, that the answer lies at the heart of what it means to be human, that "I am" unique and alive.

One of the most suggestive and insightful sequences in the film portrays a man who is attempting to create an art object out of numerous large blocks. This struggle with the aesthetic material, as the blocks leap around and even assault the artist from time to time, is accompanied by the reflections of Edison, Hemingway, and Einstein. At the conclusion of the creation, there is time for the public to make its judgment. In this sequence, there is an almost unanimous disparagement of the creative act, which is graphically portrayed in the literal shooting down of the artist by words such as "superficial," "sick," etc. And at the end comes a glimmer of hope when a woman cries out, "I don't know, I like it." But she continues, "Speaking as a mother, it seems to me that the material alone ought to be worth $100." The sequence ends leaving the distinct impression that the primary criterion of our society for creativity is its utility.

The emerging culture cries out with one voice that creativity must be valued for itself. The creative act embodies the human, and therefore it is a corruption to reduce it to any form of predetermined application. Creativity must be linked neither simply with playfulness, where one examines, sees, looks at one object and sees another, nor with the struggle of the creative process. Creativity must also be born of a joyous leap of the imagination which confirms a man's inviolable uniqueness in his creativity.

Suppression of creativity is perhaps best exemplified in much of our pedagogical and educational process. We tend to strive for a clarity and preciseness of methodology that stresses the discovery of new insights in a systematic and conceptually precise way. Yet the preoccupation with precision inhibits the creativity of those who fashion and respond freely to any creative encounter. Many a student has been so overwhelmed with his first course in any subject matter by all the delineation, detail, and drudgery that this experience decapitates any further interest in the subject. The student is often oppressed with the image of "academic pursuit." The task of consuming and analyzing information stifles his natural instincts, emotions, and sensibilities until he is sympathetic with the theme of a recent student essay, "The Student as Nigger." The authoritarian figure of the teacher and of the system not only radically inhibits natural curiosity and expression but also limits possibilities for creativity.

An instructor too frequently makes certain that the students understand the presuppositions, methodology, structure, and prescribed limits of the project at hand, almost implying that the project should be completed in terms of the instructor's presuppositions and expectations. Then, after all this proscription, he has the nerve to castigate his students for a lack of initiative and for an inability to pursue original research or manifest a creative leap of the imagination. As an instructor, I find myself too often tempted to erect secure but rigid walls of definition around the appointed topic.

This is obviously not an accurate description of all our educational procedures, nor is it intended to be a total condemnation. Analyses for the need for educational reform, however, seem to indicate that constructing "boxes" in which students must learn is far too prevalent at every level of the educational process. There are points at which this almost implicit educational presupposition is being challenged, such as in the "school without walls" which had its origin in Philadelphia. Even the practice of allowing grammar-school children to indulge in creative writing without constantly correcting their spelling and grammar accentuates the creative process and the freeing of the human imagination.

There are many areas in which a concern for the restoration of creativity could be demonstrated. However, I wish to concentrate on one particular area not only because it incorporates many of the motifs already discussed but because it has in some instances come to be identified as the characteristic phenomenon of the counter culture. This is music and particularly rock music. The topic is also significant because it has been the point of what I consider to be some rather superficial judgments about the counter culture which have been propagated by the mass media. This is exemplified in an article appearing in a recent issue of *Time* entitled "Out of Tune and Lost in the Counterculture."[9] It suggests the identification of the "counterculture" (note the form of the noun) not only with the drug culture but with a "hard" drug scene. Probably even more disturbing is what I consider to be a misleading statement: "The culture sprang more than anything else from rock-'n'-roll music." The shallowness of the interpretation is exemplified in the two basic characteristics identified. First, the "shattering, obliterating volume of electrically amplified, music, so awesomely loud it made pant legs flap and ears go numb for days." Linked to this enormous volume, which amounts to a new form of violence, is the second characteristic described as "the anarchic, brute-sexual rhythm and lyrics." Concentrating both on the volume and a particular interpretation of the lyrics may account for what I think is a rather prevalent mistake of seeing rock music as the genesis of a movement, rather than a partial expression of some more substantive motifs upon which the culture is founded.

Let me suggest first that there is a transition in the forms of music that has caused this emerging culture to light up. These forms should be seen and evaluated in a wholistic way, which includes their later and perhaps more mature manifestations. It is my assertion that music is essential to the growth and expression of the emerging culture in a way that is unique in comparison to the development of other cultures.

The cultural revolution finds its articulation in a music of unrestrained creativity and self-expression. It is this perhaps more than anything else which characterizes the music of the counter culture, particularly in folk-rock, and in the haunting ballads that appear to point the future direction of its cultural proclamations.

The claim for unrestrained creativity has its roots not simply in the fact that rock groups and individual artists have their own unique and distinctive style of dress and performance, not simply because most of the major groups and artists perform as well as compose their own music and lyrics. Most important, it evokes the participation and creativity of others who begin not only to play instruments but to compose their own music. It is not enough for people simply to listen and respond no matter how energetically or "orgy-istically." The impact of this music often presses one toward the creation and performance of music that would be an authentic self-expression of who he is. Many earlier generations have been inspired by the music of a Bach or a Mozart or a Stravinsky, but not many were so deeply moved as to spend large periods of their time actually playing musical instruments and attempting to create musically an authentic expression of their own consciousness. This factor alone might justify the significance of this new music. However, there are other factors which undergird the claim that this music gives voice to unrestrained creativity and self-expression.

The volume at which this music is played and performed might engage us first not because it is the more important point, but because it is one that sometimes draws the most attention and consternation from those seeking to understand the counter culture. The most frequent complaint is that one cannot understand the words the first time and that the volume level distracts from, if not disrupts, any other activity that might be going on, particularly within a household. The volume of the music is only one manifestation of the intent to assault the senses. When this is combined, as it often was in the earlier stages, with the flashing of images and the throbbing of strobe lights, the result was what Cox calls a "sensory overload."[10] The aim is precisely not to let the music be a pleasant addition to some other primary activity, probably a routine one such as reading, writing, cooking, cleaning, or

ACADEMIC PURSUIT

This print is available from Robert Hodgell, Box 46813, Pass-a-Grille Beach, Florida 33741

sleeping. The goal is to jolt one out of a preoccupation with routine and to catapult not only one's mind but all of his senses in a new direction, perhaps even a transcendent one. However, if one refuses to be transported and is unable to tear himself away from this preoccupation, then the resulting frustration causes not only annoyance but probably also produces a headache as well.

The music and volume are combined in an attempt to conjure up a wholistic encounter which defies that attempt to break up systematically the experience and analyze it en route. Frequently, one's inability to understand the words the first few times through affirms the idea that the primary aim is not a cognitive message embodied in the words that can be neatly apprehended and packaged. One must hear the music again and again until one is absorbed in the total experience, and the lyrics become only one component in the process of self-expression and communication.

The creative performance of the music is an attempt to confront the listener as a whole person and to begin the process of challenging his present consciousness and directing him toward other alternatives. The music often merits such confrontation even if it means that those on both sides of the culture gap must gird themselves up for the sensory assault. The music must, of course, be viewed critically, since it often is reduced to mere noise and revelry that does not merit a shift in consciousness of any kind; namely, it is not conducive to the humane.

It is, in fact, incredible that many express a desire to understand the thrust of the emerging culture and yet reject out of hand the music which is one crucial form of expression for this culture. There is, of course, some development in the music itself that now appears to be shifting much more to the ballad with the symbolic and poetic lyrics meshing and integrating with a more simplified sound reflective of the particular artist.

The early stages of folk-rock may have had as one of their purposes that of catching the attention. Yet when a growing generation was "tuned in," it then became possible to extend the medium in new directions. The full span of this development has moved from blues, or black soul music, to rock and roll, and then to folk-rock, and white soul, and now to a form of country folk music. Obviously, this is not measured progression nor are there absolute lines of distinction between the types of music involved. However, I think, this understanding does help to begin to avoid stereotyping the emerging culture with any particular kind of music and at least to be sensitive to the kinds of ways in which a vision may be expressed and interpreted through various forms of music.

I wish to suggest very briefly several other characteristics that spring from this foundation of creativity and self-expression. They are: the poetic power of the lyrics, communality, mystery, and infectious energy. As a way to illustrate them concretely, let me introduce a friend, Kathy Van der Horst. She was Kathy Gregory, prior to her marriage, and this is the name under which she has composed and recorded much of her music. She said to me in effect, "Bob, you can't have this 'head thing' by simply psyching out the message of the lyrics." As Bob Dylan notes, the word "message" strikes the young generation "as having a hernia-like sound." He goes on to claim that the only people who deliver "messages" are from Western Union.[11]

Actually, Kathy introduces herself through her own songs in the records bound together with this book. Obviously, these records will not reverberate with the best stereophonic sound; their full effect can be enjoyed through her album,

Myself.[12] They are included, however, not just because Kathy has been my own tutor in the music of this emerging culture, but because her music is symbolic of what this package involves. If your own encounter with the themes of the emerging culture is only a "head" trip, and probably a very short and dull one at that, it will have meant very little. As I noted earlier, this illustrated book, together with the records, is designed to provide a multisensory experience. Therefore, it would have been a violation of Kathy's integrity simply to print the text of the lyrics in the book and comment on them, and also it would have been a violation of my own image of what the emerging culture is demanding of us. It is demanding that we attempt to experience music, posters, prints, and games with other people in community and common commitment. And then that we attempt not simply to discuss them with each other but to respond in such a way that they are experientially shared with each other. Including the additional material will not obviously guarantee that this confrontation will occur. Genuine confrontation is an extraordinarily difficult and risky process. However, including this material at least allows for the possibility that it might serve to entice one's imagination, to stimulate honest debate, and consequently to encourage an insightful examination of one's priorities.

These songs were also included not only because of the beautiful clarity of Kathy's voice and the haunting persuasive combination of her lyrics and her tunes, but also because of what they manifest about this person. First, they manifest her own creativity; all Kathy's songs are of her own composition. These songs, in their fullness, also strive to interpret the issues and situations with which Kathy was struggling; they become her prophetic proclamation. The breadth of her capacity and concern is expressed in the ironic contrast between the probing social comment and protest on gun legislation and the lilting tune in her song, "Prepared for Killing." An exuberant joy and zest for life are expressed in "Spring in My Heart." A clear declaration of the dehumanizing and self-defeating effects of violence comes bursting forth in "After Cambodia," as if to provide a sobering perspective. This is followed by "Myself," a self-evaluative and critical examination of the often indulgent and isolationistic individual who may be found in the counter culture. "If" provides a subtle challenge to risk oneself for and with others so that life may touch and awaken one. Finally, in celebration comes the declaration of belief and the persistent testimony of the intrinsic worth of human life in all situations as evidenced in "Celebration."

But I am on the verge if not already over the line of doing what Kathy shuns—providing preset interpretation for experience with music. The words to the songs have been included in the Guide that follows these chapters to prod the conversation for those engaged in a constructive confrontation with this emerging culture. I would also hope they will be a stimulus for some who experience the songs to learn them, to sing them, and perhaps to revise them to become their own self-expression.

Kathy no doubt would not consider herself part of the "counterculture" as described and interpreted by the mass media. However, she is representative of those who authentically participate in the themes and motifs of this emerging culture. Her music appears primarily composed and sung for the sake of joy and also for shared communication. Recently, she traveled with her husband to Europe where they are preparing to carry on a ministry of service in Africa. In this new location her concern will be to use her music in order to encounter those whom she

BELIEF AND THE COUNTER CULTURE

shall serve and to share a loving relationship with them. The lyrics of the music of the emerging culture have become in some ways not only their poetry but their philosophy. As Reich suggests, they have

succeeded in expressing an understanding of the world, and of peoples' feelings, incredibly far in advance of what other media have been able to express. Journalists, writers for opinion journals, social scientists, novelists, have all tried their hand at discussing the issues of the day. But almost without exception, they have been far more superficial than the writers of rock poetry.[13]

Consider the pithy and illuminating comment of Bob Dylan on contemporary issues with his "It's All Right Ma (I'm Only Bleeding)," or in his work "Masters of War," observes the pounding critique embodied in the Fugs' song "Kill for Peace" or the meandering comments on ethics and war by Arlo Guthrie in "Alice's Restaurant Massacree." Consider a psychological or sociological analysis of the contemporary scene with the rock opera *Tommy* by The Who. To consider the hopes and desires and perhaps even the fantasies of the emerging culture for the future, one might examine the Beatles' "Yellow Submarine," or "I Feel Free" by the Cream. The mysterious and the incomprehensible has been embodied in the writing of Cohen in "Suzanne." And then, finally, there is the embodiment of the query about what it means to be human and the possible link not only with belief but also with religious commitment in the rock opera *Jesus Christ Superstar*. However, one must be reminded of Kathy's warning not to extract the words from the music lest one fragment the experience.

There is a contagious energy about the music that has a tendency to set one swaying, if not dancing and embracing his neighbor. The creative capacity of this music is in its potential for evoking responses. I recommend that you listen to Kathy's records or seek out and experience some of the other recordings noted here. An encounter with this music may provide for some a hint of the recovery of mystery and restoration of creativity which have been proclaimed here. For others, the encounter may be interpreted as an aesthetic experience that fosters sharing and a sense of community. A new consideration of this media and an attempt to interpret it may establish the music as a bridge and not a barrier across the culture gap.

Reflection on and response to mystery and creativity raise the issue of communication.

NOTES

1. Lewis Mumford, *The Myth of the Machine* (Harcourt, Brace & World, Inc., 1967), p. 286.

2. Harvey Cox, *The Feast of Fools* (Harvard University Press, 1970), p. 101.

3. William Stringfellow, *Instead of Death* (The Seabury Press, Inc., 1963), p. 16.

4. Granger Westberg, *Good Grief* (The Fortress Press, 1963), p. 18.

5. Cox, *Feast*, pp. 103-104.

6. Even in nineteenth-century United States "all of the social classes took opiates in freely available patent medicines and some members of all social classes became addicted. . . . The rate of addiction may have been higher than it is in contemporary United States" (Bernard Barber, *Drugs and Society* [Russell Sage Foundation, 1967], pp. 137-138).

7. "In the United States he [the drug addict] has been defined as a criminal and stereotyped as a 'dope fiend.' In much of Europe, on the other hand, the addict is regarded as an unfortunate person whose problem is primarily psychological and medical." (John A. Clausen, "Drug Addiction: Social Aspects" in David L. Sills [ed.], *International Encyclopedia of Social Sciences* [The Macmillan Company and The Free Press, 1968], pp. 298-299.)

8. John Carmody, S.J., "Karl Rahner: Theology of the Spiritual Life," in Martin E. Marty and Dean G. Peerman (eds.), *New Theology*, No. 7 (London: Macmillan & Company, Ltd., 1970), pp. 25-33.

9. *Time*, Feb. 22, 1971, pp. 15-16.

10. Cox, *Feast*, p. 109.

11. Nat Hentoff, "Playboy Interview: Bob Dylan," *Playboy*, March, 1966, p. 44.

12. *Myself*, by Kathy Gregory, Project III, The Total Sound, Inc., New York.

13. Charles A. Reich, *The Greening of America* (Random House, Inc., 1970), p. 247.

MYSTERY AND CREATIVITY

V

Symbols of the Vision

The expressway heading out of Chicago was unusually crowded for a Sunday morning. As my family and I were driving along in the middle lane of traffic headed south, we noticed that the man and woman in the car passing us to our left were scowling at us instead of offering the usual vacant stare. My wife and I mentioned this, but would probably not have thought much more about it, except that in the next car passing on the right the driver was not only scowling but shook his fist at us as he went by. The third car to pass contained four teen-agers who all smiled, laughed, and waved. I was thoroughly mystified until I glanced in my rearview mirror and saw my two daughters, ages five and seven, sitting in the back of the station wagon flashing the two upraised fingers of the peace sign to each car that approached from the rear. It was quite clear that they were relaying something to the occupants of the other cars, and getting quite a variety of responses to a rather provocative symbolic form of communication. This illustrates in a very commonplace way the problems of communication and the crucial role of cultural symbols. Obviously, two little girls could not be readily identified with a cultural revolution. Just as obviously their sign language was interpreted in such a way that it drew quite divergent reactions.

Communication stands at the very center of what it means to be human. Communication allows one to be bound with other people in communities of support and renewal. Also, authentic dialogue with other persons allows one to clarify his own visions, to determine his own priorities, and thus ultimately to develop an authentic mode of living. Yet human communication has an element of mystery about it. Communication in this sense is not the transfer of ideas but a "sharing" between two individuals, a speaker and a hearer. It is the sharing of mutual understanding about some aspect of their experience or world, about some aspect of that which constitutes reality for them. Our language, when communication actually occurs, provides an access to or lights up a certain aspect of reality that is now available to both the speaker and the hearer through the medium of language. It should be made clear, however, that communication as a "shared understanding" has a context that is much wider than just the linguistic.

The emerging culture has accused the dominant society of being hung up on its rhetoric, of being a society trapped within its own slogans.

BELIEF AND THE COUNTER CULTURE

It is a society that shows an enormous discrepancy between declarations and delivery. Many in the dominant culture illustrate this discrepancy in their distinction between private and public standards of ethical responsibility. A member of one of my study seminars, who characterized herself as part of the Establishment, was extraordinarily disturbed by the implication that Jerry Rubin had managed to avoid some income-tax payments on a portion of his royalties for the book *Do It: Scenarios of the Revolution*. However, she saw no parallel between this alleged activity and the process whereby large corporations through legal loopholes and tax write-offs avoid hundreds of times the amount of taxation evaded by Rubin. A man who commits a robbery for himself and his family under the duress of poverty, or even more illustrative, the man who is caught with the possession of a marijuana cigarette is certainly subject to arrest and imprisonment. In contrast, public officials, particularly in places of power, may engage in large-scale public theft in the form of graft and corruption and may risk only a reprimand or, at worst, dismissal.

It is apparent, however, that the charge of discrepancy is also applicable on the other side of the culture gap. The young proclaim quite clearly their freedom and independence from the repressive requirements of an affluent technocracy but are often quite ready to receive direct assistance from this affluence in the form of parental checks. One of the busiest places in town is the General Delivery section of the post office in the area of Big Sur, where the free children come to collect their periodic checks from home. And those who vociferously protest the ecological crisis produced by irresponsible pollutants continue to drive automobiles, buy nonreturnable bottles, and cause pollution at rock festivals that staggers one's imagination.

Authentic communication is not foiled by a lack of words, but because these words are not received in a context that produces mutual sharing and a kind of trust. The context for communication is crucial, since it provides the basis for authentic dialogue. This is well illustrated by the repetition in one of my seminars by a young person and in another by a member of the Establishment of the old saying, "Your actions speak so loudly I can't hear what you say."

The notion of communication, of "rapping," of "being heard," and of getting through is almost an obsession with the young and particularly with those in the counter culture. In the study seminars which I have conducted on this topic we usually engage in some activities to test one's listening capacity. As an introductory process, I frequently go around the group, asking each member to share with some frankness the reason why he decided to participate in the seminar and also to tell the group one characteristic, interest, or quality that would identify him to the group. At the conclusion of this process it is then suggested that we go back around the group and have each one indicate the distinguishing characteristics of the other members of the group. The immediately apparent and somewhat startling fact is that almost no one in the group is able to do this. Subsequent reflection and confession reveal that this is not so much the result of a faulty memory as one's absolute preoccupation with what he is going to say about himself, which blocks any real capacity to listen to the other.

It is my conviction that with terrifying frequency this is precisely what happens within our culture. We are so busy preparing our own response to an important and particularly threatening question that we immediately project our own presuppositions and concerns upon those persons to whom we are listening. The result is that even though we hear the words, there is no real shared understanding that lights up some aspect of our experience.

This lack of communication is said to result in a so-called generation gap where one is alienated from his parents and from others who do not share his vision of himself and his world. Not only do they not share this vision, too often they do not even really recognize or understand it. Therefore, many young people feel that this failure in communication is rooted in an alienation at the core of human development. The young person sees himself as alienated from the established culture, from his environment, and even from himself, or at least the vision of the free self he desires to be. Often a young person participating in the seminar complains that other participants are lecturing him or treating his judgments paternalistically and condescendingly rather then taking them at face value as an expression of his belief and commitment. However, as I have argued, this sense of frustration is not the result of an age differential, but rather a vision differential which is based on how one feels about himself and his world. It should be noted that significant communication does not depend on a transformation in consciousness—only on the ability to appreciate different cultural perspectives.

The problem of alienation is more complex than simply a lack of communication. As Theodore Roszak reminds us, Herbert Marcuse and Norman O. Brown both agree that such a fundamental form of alienation perhaps characteristic of both parent and child is primarily psychic and not sociological.[1] The power to overcome this sense of alienation may rest in a changed consciousness, a new perception of one's self and of others. There can be a sudden shock of recognition not only about what one is now but about what he might be in the future. What is required, then, to dispel this sense of alienation which, I think, is prevalent on both sides of the culture gap is a "therapeutic revolution" that will transform consciousness and life-style. This revolution might be understood as the expenditure of human energy that ultimately rests in a change in the life-style of a majority of the people in a given culture. For the emerging culture, the guide to illumination is not research but vision.

The future of a rehumanized culture is linked to just such a transformation of consciousness. This alteration in mind-set is affected neither initially nor even primarily by reasoned argumentation supported by evidence, but rather by the reception of illuminating and transforming cultural symbols. Reflect for a moment on how people change their minds, or even more specifically, how one changes his mind about a particular idea, activity, or person. Is it primarily on the basis of new information or data, carefully weighed until the balance scale of one's mind suddenly tips to the other side? Is this the way a person decides whether he will oppose or support the war in Vietnam, whether he will make a shift in vocation, or whether he likes his daughter's new boyfriend? My own experience indicates that major decisions about events or people are made on the basis of sudden flashes of insight, new experiences, or even fresh intuitions. This sudden change of mind, this conversion, is not unrelated to evidence, data, and information, but more than likely it finds justification and confirmation only later after the decision has been made and the position must be bolstered and defended. A new mind-set is more like seeing things through new glasses than like dropping the last tiny weight onto the scales of judgment.

Some people do, of course, make their decisions on the basis of accruing data, objectively observing the results, and pursuing the consequences of that process. It is my judgment, however, that this is rare, particularly when it comes to issues of cultural and personal transformation. Rather, such decisions are linked to something that could be characterized in terms of a "conversion" or a "re-formation." In this process the cultural symbol plays a pivotal and determinative role.

It should be clear that symbol is employed here in a very special sense. It is not reduced simply to a functional representation. For example, a doctor uses ♀ as a symbol in a medical report or a psychological study of a woman. This is a sign or a signal simply intended to make one think of the term "woman" or "female." In contrast, the symbol 卐 arouses for many people a host of negative feelings and painful images. "Symbol" is used in this analysis in a special way to refer to something, either a word or object or sound, that makes what it symbolizes come alive in your experience. In other words, a symbol causes you to encounter something mentally and emotionally. As F. W. Dillistone puts it, a symbol is "that which points toward, shares in, and in some way conforms to, a reality which cannot be fully expressed through any descriptive languages or visual forms already available to us."[2] The symbol not only incorporates and integrates past experience, but also gives us new insights and expands our awareness.

I wish to call this special use of symbol "illuminating" and "transforming" because this understanding of symbol suggests that something is really lighted up or changed. Symbol has a special kinship to that to which it points, making that event or experience really present and alive to those in a given community who understand and employ the symbol. Thus the flag of a nation, a peace symbol, the hammer and sickle, a star of David, a dove, a cross, may cause one to respond in a negative, positive, or neutral way, depending on how these are employed. The response is evoked because the symbols cause one to participate in the experience. It is some of these symbols and the different reactions they evoke which we want to examine more carefully.

Key symbols have implications for the way in which one lives his life. Therefore, symbols are developed and projected in the form of a myth that tells a story about how a person will react or how a community will respond. Myth is not a reference here to something that is untrue, but rather to an imaginative and creative construction of the specific living through of a particular experience. So a myth developed of the pioneer or frontiersman, of the concerned father, of the enterprising executive, of the creative artist, of the compassionate mother, of the devoted son, and even of the Boy Scout. Langdon Gilkey maintains that every symbol or myth entails a model for existence. "And since no culture can exist without forms of human excellence by which life is guided . . . even secular culture lives by its religious myths and images of man."[3]

There is particularly within the counter culture a concern for what I shall describe as "symbolic consciousness." The "new consciousness" with which the counter culture is preoccupied is the result of an interaction with experience. This experience, I suggest, is so affected by certain creative symbols that it is described as symbolic consciousness. How does the symbol operate in this process? Rollo May, a noted psychotherapist, asserts that symbols have two psychological functions. First, "they are man's way of expressing the quintessence of his experience—his way of seeing his life, his self-image, and his relations to the world of his fellowmen and of nature." Secondly, they embody "the vital meaning of his experience."[4] Symbols, as they are woven into a story or myth, shape our consciousness and ultimately determine the way in which we act, our life-style.

How are symbols received? How does one come to adopt certain symbols as being operative for him? In stable cultural periods symbols are bequeathed to its young by the society and reinforced by a majority of its members. The key symbols are enshrined within and inculcated by the educational system and the economic structure. Those who accept, support, and embody the symbols are rewarded appropriately by the society. Religious institutions and public mores tend to undergird and extend the symbols. The family unit at one time was the major component of society where symbols were introduced and interpreted. These symbols of motherhood, patriotism, manhood, justice, etc., are declared by society and then molded into myths of accepted forms of behavior. However, we have suggested that something becomes an operative myth, an operative symbol, only when it is received as such, namely, only when it actually functions to coordinate, integrate, and guide one's human experience. The symbol is then, we have noted, received as a result of the interaction of the individual with experience. Part of the socializing thrust of the society is precisely to inculcate and reinforce its own predominant symbols and therefore patterns of life.

In periods of cultural sterility these central symbols and myths are still declared. The difference is that they are not actually received; they fail to have the persuasive power to become embodied as a result of one's encounter with experience. This lack of receptivity is often most evident among the young. What develops is a growing sense of uncertainty and confusion, expressions of alienation, lack of communication, and crisis. The symbols of a society are no longer authentic, functioning symbols because they have lost their potency.

In periods of cultural revolution, symbols and myths of the dominant culture are challenged, rejected, and often actively attacked. Simultaneously, new symbols and myths are envisioned and articulated. They arise out of an active period of exploration in which new options are examined. Out of this process of experimentation the new symbols begin to take form and are received as authentic. If the cultural revolution succeeds, then it is these symbols and motifs which become embodied in a multiplicity of ways in order to form the new culture.

I believe we find ourselves teetering between the recognition of a sterile and impotent culture, one that does not really provide transforming and illuminating symbols that give authenticity to life, and the emergence of a new culture, where new and vibrant symbols and myths have not yet been received by a majority of the society. The crisis is generally felt and often articulated precisely in terms of a cultural revolution. The unusual thing about this situation is that many seem to be extraordinarily self-conscious about what is taking place. Perhaps what is more unusual is the sensitivity to the force of the symbolic embodiment of new values and new guidelines for the culture.

A rather striking confirmation of this cultural pattern occurs in the work of the psychoanalyst Rollo May. He indicates that in recent years when a patient indicated that he had nothing to believe in anymore, one could assume that the difficulty lay within an unconscious conflict in symbols. This conflict might take the form of "mother and protectiveness" or "God and the authoritarian father." A therapeutic task, then, was to assist the patient to work through the conflict in symbols in order that he might choose his own and find in it a sense of direction. However, beginning in the late fifties, at least with more sophisticated patients, the problem changed. Apparently there has been such a deterioration in cultural symbols that the problem no longer focused on a conflict in symbols. Rather, patients were unable to find any symbols at all by which to integrate and orient their minds. There was and is a sense of meaninglessness in the vacuity of any symbols strong enough to draw one's commitment. There was in the late fifties simply a sense of futility. The situation was so sterile that May suggests that many patients were even unable to discover a symbol within the culture which justified fighting against. May goes on to suggest that this deterioration of symbols was not restricted to patients in psychotherapy but was so widespread that it now percolates down throughout the members of society.[5] This situation which emerged in the fifties found wide confirmation throughout the culture by the late sixties. This vacuum in symbols has been filled by techniques, tools, and methods. We are preoccupied now with the study of process and of the techniques or methods that facilitate an appropriate process. Interests range from new business studies on organizational behavior to sensitivity training for middle executives in order that they can better relate to one another and to their subordinates, and even to the study of techniques in sexual relations. The latter has been carried to ridiculous lengths in a best seller *The Sensuous Woman,* which emphasizes training, exercise, and techniques as the clue to sexual relations. Obviously, some concern with process, method, and even techniques is quite appropriate, but these cannot be substitutes for genuine personal symbols which provide the power for the integration and orientation of human life around a new vision. May's analysis appeared a few years ago, but our present situation is comparable in that man has tended to take on the image of a program-

med automaton which adjusts to certain demands of the culture.

What man lacks is a symbol or myth that could tranform his life into a creative and exciting adventure. What distinguishes our situation, however, from that about which May as a psychoanalyst was writing is that new myths and symbols now are emerging. A new sensitivity to the symbolic dimension within the counter culture is a manifestation of the quest for and the promise of a new appreciation for transforming and illuminating symbols that may emerge and very slowly be accepted and adopted by communities.

The perceptive studies of Roszak, Novak, or Reich stress the inadequacy of present cultural symbols that embody the priorities of the contemporary society. Some of the present symbols are: status mirrored in titles, public recognition, and material rewards; individualism enshrined in a highly competitive attitude that is reflected in every aspect of society; American nationalism, which has tended to identify human interest with the national interest of the corporate state; efficiency, which puts a premium on the use of time, so that one is simply unable to function without a watch; and productivity, which characterizes human worth by what one does and not by what he is. These key symbols around which one's life is at least implicitly oriented have their own verbal or visual images. These are exemplified, for instance, in one's salary range, home, or automobile, in title or position, in competitive scales such as grades, sales record, or promotion schedule, the clock and the computer, the ever-present dossier needed for education, occupation, and even for a bank loan. These cultural images finally become capsulized in the obituary.

We cannot pause for a detailed analysis of the cultural symbols noted here, and in fact an analysis would be inappropriate in abstraction. Rather, their adequacy will, I think, emerge in constructive confrontation, particularly as they are placed in juxtaposition with the new symbols for the emerging culture. It should be made clear that there is no attempt here to prejudge these out of hand, but only to illustrate that they are precisely the symbols which the emerging culture is challenging. More and more individuals within the dominant society are confessing that these images and myths do not function as transforming or illuminating symbols. They are dying symbols because they fail to integrate or orient human experience. These symbols do not expand awareness or provide insight. They generate no vision.

Let me provide only one other illustration for the sake of reflection. A student of mine, William Weber, argued that it is in television and particularly in advertising that the implicit symbols and myths of a society are utilized, precisely because they sell products. In order to make this thesis more apparent, he compiled a half-hour film composed of commercials spliced together with some still shots from the news interspersed between them. (This contrast indicated the proportionate amount of TV time invested in commercials over against a consideration of news events or their analysis.) The intent of the project was to illustrate that commercial messages consistently placed a primary emphasis on performance and productivity. It was repeatedly implied that the viewer as consumer must also perform or "measure up."

This is true whether you are a business executive, construction worker, housewife, or new breed of lawyer or physician, long hair and all. Man is portrayed as needing above all a sense of success and accomplishment, which results in status, material rewards, and perhaps even more important, in acceptance, romance, love,

and even freedom. Reflect on the key symbols suggested above and see if they are not precisely enshrined in television ads for automobiles, deodorants, toothpastes, perfume, aftershave lotion, airlines, and even dog food, where it is suggested that one put himself in the place of his dog.

The emerging culture has for the most part rejected the function of the mass media as not only demeaning and corrupting but actually manipulating in the guise of entertainment. However, if television commercials become a way to make us self-conscious about the myths and symbols we have promoted but now wish to question, then they are perhaps serving a useful function. This is perhaps comparable to the way in which widespread publicity on the war in Vietnam has sensitized people to the question of the nature of the country's involvement and commitment to this venture and perhaps even more to the staggering loss of human life that it has reaped.

The concern for communication epitomized in the emerging culture is, I think, exemplified in the effort to demonstrate the nature of this cultural revolution. To be sure, a primary concern for the emerging culture is simply in experimenting with and developing new and truly authentic life-styles. However, closely following this is the emphasis on joyously and freely sharing symbols, myths, and modes of living that have become liberating and fulfilling for those who have adopted them. Perhaps the best way to speak to this interest is not in abstraction and thus again to negate the experiential in the name of the theoretical. Nor is the most light shed on a cultural revolution by examining its extremes, i.e., those who have completely separated themselves from the dominant society or those who in excessive reaction reject all new options. The latter proclaim that there is really no crisis and staunchly defend traditional values and priorities against any attack. The most fruitful area for investigation is neither the far out nor the far back, but rather, I think, is with people who are trying to struggle with issues and communicate with each other. These persons are those who recognize the crisis, confess their own confusion, and are seeking a vision—whether that means a revitalization of one already present or the articulation of a new one. Hope is invested in those who seek to be, however tenuously, in communication with each other about the future of our culture and our life together and about the issue of what it means to be human. This attitude has with some exceptions been characteristic of the seminars on this topic that I participated in throughout the United States. It is from this concrete context that I would like to introduce the issue of transforming and illuminating symbols.

What might the role be of those who are sensitive to the crisis within the culture in the next few years? Primarily, I think, it will be their role to envision and elucidate the symbols and visions that will transform our sense of reality, our consciousness. Michael Novak, in his book *The Experience of Nothingness*, follows May's analysis with a declaration of what we require in the new myth: "We stand in need of a new sense of reality, a new image of how to be intelligent, sensitive, and free."[6] My difficulty with Novak's proposal, if I understand it correctly, is that man is to create or invent his symbols or myths. Man does, according to Novak, continually invent the self. However, this does not seem to be a very promising way of arriving at an ultimately more authentic or humanizing symbol or myth than we have at the present. Man tends to create that which he wishes to believe. I would prefer to speak of discovering symbols, for transforming and illuminating symbols are the consequence of an encounter, a transaction between man and experience, between an individual and that reality which is the ground of his own life and existence. It is this reality which many within the emerging culture wish to confess as the transcendent, or God. Therefore, authentic cultural symbols are revealed or discovered more than invented or created. Constructive confrontations where people are linked by a common human concern become the context for the discovery of these new symbols.

On occasion, symbols get hung up or caught between two cultural movements. Both sides of the culture gap employ the symbol but invest it with different meanings. It represents for each a different vision. It may be instructive to consider one of them in order to observe the ironic way in which symbols function and illustrate why they often demand interpretation. We suggested previously that poster art and certain forms of music are primary means of symbolic communication precisely because they elicit a more pluralistic human response. Poster art in particular often thrives on double meaning and illustrates a subtle use of irony.

The poster *We Can't Let It Die* was one of the most controversial posters of the twenty-five or thirty used regularly within my study seminars on the counter culture. Many of the older people, but by no means all, were highly offended by the poster because they saw the flag, and by implication the nation, being demeaned and ridiculed. Many of the younger people in the seminar, but by no means all, understood the poster to make a satirical comment on the death-producing stance of the nation presently, but saw it primarily as a positive comment on the possibility of reviving the original roots of the nation's heritage. This poster dramatizes the present conflict that is coursing through the society over the American flag.

Many are infuriated when an American flag

is burned, particularly at a public demonstration, since it is an incineration vicariously of their own commitments and visions for their country. Often in reaction people then begin to display the flag not only on public holidays but regularly, to put flag decals on their car windows or to attach miniature flags to their aerials. In contradistinction to this, the flag also has become material for shirts, pants, bikinis, and even bed sheets (or at least the flag has inspired the design). But perhaps more important the flag has become a symbol to wear on not only the sleeve of a leather jacket but also on the seat of the pants of some rather rugged members of motorcycle gangs. The irony of this appeared in a conversation I had with a "bikie" at a rock festival. He was displaying an American flag sewed to the seat of his pants. When I asked if that was a way for him to make fun of the flag and the nation, he replied, "No, man, I love this country." And while patting his rear, he exclaimed, "It's basic!" The bikie went on to explain in his own distinctive vocabulary that he was committed to the country's recovering its foundation which had in fact been revolutionary. He strongly supported the ideals of freedom of expression, particularly criticism, freedom of opportunity for all, and the freedom for life, liberty, and the pursuit of happiness for each individual or community as they defined it. However, this was only as long as those freedoms didn't, as he expressed it, "cream the rights of others." This new manifestation of patriotism is vividly stated in another poster which declares: "Don't burn the flag. Wash it!"

The flag has been displayed for many purposes. As was noted in one of my southern seminars, it is sometimes employed to counter the sectionalism involved in the display of the Confederate flag alone. The point I wish to make is that the flag illustrates the conflict of a symbol precisely because it represents different visions of the nation and its future. One vision stresses self-reliance, pride, opportunity for advancement, a sense of defending our own rights and the rights of those who ally themselves with us—the sense of unity for a common cause. The other vision highlights the theme of freedom, of plurality, of a nation where no man's mouth or mind may be bound, and where we should not arbitrarily impose our will on others. There is a sense of lostness and betrayal on both sides, although I do not think it means that these visions are necessarily contradictory. Regardless of how the vision is specifically sketched, it is very clear that it demands interpretation.

The symbol, I have suggested, has the potential to affect and to shape the consciousness in a way that cannot be replaced by information. Thus the interpretation of the symbol cannot be substituted for the power of the symbol to make an experience come alive for a person or for a community. The interpretation is intended to liberate another person to apprehend the symbol and its power. For example, the work of a literary critic can never provide a substitute for an encounter with a poem or a narrative. His task is to facilitate our aesthetic experience with the work of art. The critic strives to make the reader open to the mode in which the poem speaks. The emphasis on communication is founded on an attempt to provide a context in which symbols can be interpreted and unpacked. The interpretation of the symbol seeks to liberate us from our biases and preconceptions. At least this interpretive process may cause us to recognize the power of a symbol for another person. Recognition allows one to consider in dialogue and sharing how that symbol might become an illuminating and transforming symbol for him. However, how do we know whether a symbol is still alive and viable for the con-

WE CAN'T LET IT DIE

sciousness of a given community? The aim of symbolic interpretation is to clarify a vision, not to create or control it.

Considering now representative symbols of the emerging culture, let me return to the image with which I began this chapter. Peace! As a song or an uttered word, as a communal gesture or inscribed as a graphic design, this has been represented in a thousand different mediums, from snow sculpture to stained glass. This is an integrating and orienting symbol for the new culture. The graphic form ☮ seems to have had its origin in England as early as 1958 during the "Ban the Bomb" movement, which focused on the question of nuclear disarmament. It is transcribed from the flag formation in semaphore language standing for "N.D.," or nuclear disarmament. The two extended fingers incorporated in a gesture have also become a distinctive peace sign in the United States. This is identified with opposition to the Vietnam war. Initially, its aim was to declare publicly and symbolically one's stance on the war and thus it came to symbolize a special bond, a special relationship to all those who shared this stance. Also, as our earlier illustration made clear, it had a tendency to put off those who did not share this sentiment about the Vietnam war.

The poster *Peace Policeman* comes from an unposed photograph taken in the city of Chicago not long after the 1968 Democratic National Convention. This poster has also been quite controversial in my seminars. Many of the young people, but by no means all, have interpreted the poster as a huge "put-on and put-down," and many refused to believe it was unposed. For them the poster jeopardizes a stereotype of the policeman as the sign of an authority that not only agrees with but enforces the Establishment position on the war. It is even more threatening because the peace sign has come to be symbolic

of much more than an attitude toward the war. It is increasingly the orienting symbol for a whole way of life. Many rejected the poster because they believed a policeman was incapable of sharing in that kind of commitment and lifestyle. Therefore, it is useful in questioning a stereotype that had tended to dehumanize policemen and protesters alike. There is an irony to this poster as well which seems to declare that the new motifs and themes of a lifestyle associated with peace are not exclusively the possession of the young or those who dissent from all aspects of the life of the dominant culture.

"Peace," "Pax," "Shalom," expressed in many other tongues or flashed as a sign, have become a form of greeting, of benediction, and a parting blessing for the emerging culture. The peace sign is displayed on the front of garage doors, flown from the top of flagpoles, worn as an emblem around the necks of men and women alike, and used at the conclusion of letters. The widespread utilization of one symbol would seem out of all proportion if it were representative only of an attitude toward the Vietnam war or perhaps toward war in general. Rather, as I am suggesting, it has become the sign for a whole new lifestyle.

Peace has a multiplicity of meanings and it would be extremely difficult even to suggest their gamut. However, for the counter culture, "peace" is not limited to the cessation of armed conflict. Neither is it limited to individual tranquillity even when one finds himself in the midst of external disruption. It is not to be identified simply with peace of mind. However, these are all component factors in the new life-style. The root meaning of the word "peace," in relationship to its Hebrew counterpart "shalom," which is being employed more and more within the emerging culture, refers to wholeness, health,

PEACE POLICEMAN

and security.[7] It speaks first of all of the wholeness of man. To be committed to peace is a healing process that restores man not only to a sense of individual integrity and harmony where one "has his head together," but it also bespeaks a relationship of communion between and among men, nature, and the transcendent. It is not only a state of mind but a state of existence where the legitimate claims and needs of all are met.

Peace is the symbolic embodiment of a vision of the emerging culture. It is this, however, because it is above all a communal term. It binds men together instead of releasing them and separating them to go their own individual and isolationist ways. Peace in this sense speaks of justice and human well-being. It points to bodily health as a factor of wholeness and also to a level of security and prosperity that frees men from dehumanizing deprivation. But perhaps most of all it envisions lives that contain individual happiness and commitment to mutuality. It rejects competitiveness which forces one to contest another until he either wins or loses. Rather, peace points to a supportive sharing that frees both persons to be authentic and to stretch toward their own fulfillment and not the satisfaction of the expectations of another. Peace as a lifestyle calls for gentleness over against aggressiveness and ambition. It summons one to a receptive humility which understands the essence of one's own intrinsic human worth and that of others. This humility makes unnecessary a demonstrative pride that must declare, must prove, one's human worth by what he does.

There is also a mysterious aspect to peace. Not many within the emerging culture envision the condition of peace to be that which they can create alone. Certainly peace must be sought as a promise, as a hope, but it is also a gift. It is a gracious gift for which one is not only joyous but thankful. It is precisely this gracious gift of the transcendent that must concern us presently. But peace is also a communal symbol which suggests that no man may fully experience the state of peace with all its hope and promise unless all know and share it. The vision of peace challenges us to discover new forms of community that will nurture and protect our experience of peace.

There are other key symbols that one might explicate, such as love, joy, and beauty. They all have special verbal and visual images that become centers around which human experience is not only oriented but also shared or communicated to another. Peace was selected not only because it is a predominant image, a predominant symbol within the emerging culture, but perhaps because it serves along with love as the central integrating factor in the cultural revolution. As the embodiment of a vision, it becomes representative of a way of living that orients one's priorities. Peace, as it has been explicated here, is interpreted by the emerging culture as an indispensable element in what it means to be human.

An experience of three young men stands out vividly in my mind. They had carefully and prayerfully thought about their opposition to a war which they considered dehumanizing for those on either side of the battle line. Therefore, they had decided to refuse induction into the armed services and to volunteer for alternative service in a more humane capacity. They were prepared, however, to sacrifice and take whatever consequences were necessary as determined by the society of which they were a part. On the day they were to announce their decision they conducted a worship service at the induction center in order to attempt to communicate to others the reasons for this stance. Following the service, as they were giving themselves up to federal authorities, an agent asked one of the young men, "What do you want?" He replied simply, "Peace." The response came in cynical tones, "What do you really want, friend?" The boy replied, "If you have peace, what else is there?" The federal agent's face suddenly softened, and he replied, "You know, son, you may be right." This was the beginning of the communication of a vision.

NOTES

1. Theodore Roszak, *The Making of a Counter Culture* (Anchor Book, Doubleday & Company, Inc., 1969), p. 95.

2. F.W. Dillistone (ed.), *Myth and Symbol* (London: S.P.C.K., 1966), p. vii.

3. Langdon Gilkey, *Naming the Whirlwind: The Renewal of God-Language* (The Bobbs-Merrill Company, Inc., 1969), p. 293.

4. Rollo May, "The Significance of Symbols," in Rollo May (ed.), *Symbolism in Religion and Literature* (George Braziller, Inc., 1959), p. 34.

5. *Ibid.*, pp. 22-24.

6. Michael Novak, *The Experience of Nothingness* (Harper & Row, Publishers, Inc., 1970), p. 106.

7. Indebtedness for this interpretation is to be attributed to my colleague Jack L. Stotts. See his perceptive analysis of the theological context for "Shalom" in *Environment and Theology* (Department of Church and Society, Board of Christian Education, The United Presbyterian Church U.S.A., 1971), pp. 8-11.

VI
Community and the Transcendent

The father in the family is later than usual in getting home from work. His wife persistently prods him to hurry and get dressed or they will be late. A good-humored hustle is being applied by the mother to her son, a college sophomore home for the weekend. She makes preparations to go out with a kind of silent, plodding resignation. After considerable negotiation father, mother, and son say good night to a teen-aged daughter, who has other plans for the evening, and hurry to the car. They drive a short distance and conversation consists of a few muted complaints by the father about whether attending this kind of thing isn't more of a hassle than it's worth. The son reminds his mother that he has agreed to come because the event is indirectly for him, but he can stay for only a little while and must get away very soon. They arrive at the home of friends where the event of the evening is already in progress. A cocktail party has been planned to meet several social needs: to say good-by to the Thompsons, who are moving to California; to hear from the Craigs about their vacation in the Bahamas; and to welcome Tom home for Thanksgiving vacation from college in the East. The context for this cultural event is set.

Change the details and allow your own memory to transplant you into the situation. After the first exuberant greetings, what happens? A number of isolated entities move around the room, bouncing off one another like billiard balls after the initial break. Each individual engages in conversation until it either gets too boring or too threatening, and then he moves on to the great goody table at the top of the room. The event thrives on superficial pleasantness, the avoidance of controversy, and inhibits any real sustained involvement and commitment to another. It is a community ritual, but one must ask himself whether it is a ritual that has any real meaning or significance.

"A cocktail party is a liturgical dramatization of our culture," suggests Michael Novak,[1] and before him, T. S. Eliot. The cocktail party, which many claim to hate and yet feel compelled to give or attend, is a mockery of community. The poster *Cocktail Chatter* depicts vividly what we not only subconsciously fear but also feel in these cultural encounters. Too often we do not experience authentic dialogue with a group of friends; rather, we perform a "duelogue" in which people appear primarily interested in shooting down one another. Instead of listening, opponents are busy reloading. The only realities exchanged here are volleys.

BELIEF AND THE COUNTER CULTURE

The consciousness of alienation prevalent among the young, but evident throughout society, is often attributed to a lack of communication. This awareness fosters a desperate search for a sense of community, a revitalization of communal trust, commitment, and support. If the cocktail party strikes you as a somewhat inappropriate portrayal of our culture, select another communal gathering such as a neighborhood tea or a coffee hour, a dinner party or even a family reunion, a fraternity beer bust or high school prom, a civic club meeting or the blast at the union hall. In the very midst of these events, however, many of us at one time or another experience this feeling of isolation and separation from those we call "friends" and even from family members. This "solitariness," many in the counter culture declare, is the result of a cultural phenomenon they label "pseudoindividualism." This has produced and been reinforced by a society dominated by self-centered, highly competitive egos. Is it really surprising that we are hesitant to reveal important concerns and strong emotions to our friends and spouses? The problem is equally evident in our inability to reveal ourselves to general acquaintances, even in so-called communities such as the church, social cliques, or civic clubs. Is our reticence surprising, since so much of life is constructed on the pattern of a huge "diplomacy" game where we succeed at the cost of an opponent's error or failure? Any indiscretion makes us vulnerable and thus the culture trains us not to get involved in other people's lives, not to risk an act that would make us a target for another's sarcastic stab or put-down.

Present educational patterns offer striking illustrations of this highly competitive, threatening, and depersonalized rivalry. Higher education constitutes one long competitive war for grades, dormitory rooms, dating partners, and most ludicrous of all, study carrels. Take, for example, the characteristic advanced college seminar. It is my observation that a student often waits until a classmate makes what he judges to be an error. He than thunders in with a crushing critique, and glances sideways to make sure his professor is observing and appreciating this demonstration of critical competence. In contrast, a critique could be offered in such a way that the critic bears specific responsibility for sketching out constructive alternatives. Consider which of the two approaches could mold the class into a communal, supportive, and contributive educational unit. The latter model is a component in the educational revolution.

One of the myths that is espoused by the dominant culture is the benefit of competition—almost its unqualified value. The educational system is founded on competition where academic class standing in some institutions is figured down to the last detail. This attitude is buttressed by the notion of intercollegiate competitive athletics. Competitive zeal is even more generously rewarded in the field of business and management. In one of my seminars, there were several executives from IBM who were quite disturbed that the new emerging culture was disparaging a competitiveness which they interpreted as being at the root of American industrial success. However, the issue that some of the other participants in the seminar pushed, not just the young, was the question of competition "At what price?"

Competition with another on a particular problem or issue could be evaluated, of course, as stimulating and encouraging in such a way as to allow one to fulfill and satisfy more adequately his own human capacity. However, far too often the competitive process has focused on only one goal—to win or to succeed. Man's desire to succeed has resulted in his minimizing and on oc-

COCKTAIL CHATTER

casion completely ignoring all values and standards, including those of humanization. Competitive pressure seems to demand that one get the contract by any means the cultural climate will tolerate. Not only has there been a lack of consideration of the human consequences for one's competition but an actual drive toward destroying the competition. In many instances this competitive drive has not actually benefited the consumer. To have fifteen types of paper toweling rather than three from which to choose is not clearly an unmitigated human benefit. Competition has induced companies to invest millions in advertisements to "create" a market where none existed. On other occasions, particularly in the automotive industry, new ideas in engine design involving lower fuel consumption or the longevity of tires were actually suppressed because they might inhibit competition and therefore sales. Competition is not an incidental factor in the drives toward planned obsolescence and maximized consumption. Individual and competitive thrusts have tended to dampen many cooperative ventures, not only between industries, particularly in the area of research, but also between nations. However, perhaps the greatest problem is that there seems to be no standard, no criterion of the human, by which to evaluate the extremes of the competitive mentality.

This competition-oriented mentality may well have its foundation in an image of man that is ingrained in our consciousness. It proclaims the uniqueness of the individuality of man, but treats him as an instrument or a tool to be employed in the fulfillment of one's desires. Our relationships to others, even friendships, are founded on the basis of our needs and interests. But this is only an outgrowth of the procedure where man treats himself as a tool and founds his self-estimation upon what he has accomplished, rather than upon what he is. The criterion for work is doing, not being. There is no possibility for intrinsic self-worth. Thus man braces himself emotionally to be shot down for what he does. It is little wonder that we fail to trust each other, that we feel isolated and alienated.

In recent years many social critics have tended to place the blame for this feeling of alienation and isolation at the door of a technological and bureaucratic society. The implication is that people feel isolated and dehumanized, primarily in their work, as the result of a populous and highly computerized society. This was epitomized in the title of a study some years ago by the sociologist David Riesman, *The Lonely Crowd.*[2] This feeling of isolation was described aptly by the Jewish philosopher Martin Buber as "mass or collective loneliness."[3] Many felt that this isolation and alienation occurred primarily in one's professional or vocational life and, with the exception of the plight of the singles, the feeling was compensated for within the family structure itself. There has been precisely for this reason an extraordinary amount of pride and self-justification for the nuclear family unit in American life.

However, what is becoming more and more evident, particularly for those who serve as pastors, psychiatrists, or professional counselors, is that not only is this sense of isolation and alienation not mitigated in the life-style of many family units, but it is in fact intensified. Not only is there an enormous amount of sibling rivalry, but implicit and explicit pressure is applied by parents to children and children to parents to "measure up" to the status demands of the society. Therefore, family units become highly competitive entities in their own right. One makes comparisons between the value and quality of possessions, the age at which children begin to walk, the intellectual, athletic, and musical prowess of a son or daughter, the degree to which a family member, whether it be mother, father, son, or daughter, accommodates himself to the expectations of the society. The family becomes highly competitive not only among its members but also among family units themselves.

Often it becomes necessary to develop images or masks that represent an individual not only to the world beyond the family but even to other family members. There is a dearth of authentic and honest sharing and communication among members of the same family. Therefore, a characteristic remark by young people in my study seminar goes something like this, "I couldn't possibly share that with my parents; they would be too disappointed and hurt." A corresponding statement by a father, less often publicly admitted, runs like this, "If I shared my mistakes and my doubts with my son, he would never respect me." Too often we build and hide behind an elaborate facade which not only inhibits but prohibits any real intimacy. This has generated, I believe, much of the discussion of a so-called "generation gap" which reflects a crisis not only in the family but in personal relationships. The crisis emerges as an absence of community, and community is perhaps man's greatest need after food and shelter.

The number of runaways is spiraling, even from homes that young people describe as stable and accepting. Increasing numbers of young people simply are "splitting" from the traditional family structure. Many are calling into question the nuclear family as a viable form for recovering the human. We indicated previously that one of the primary themes of the emerging culture was a rediscovery of the self, but this was a self in community. The counter culture is persuaded that a sense of community is essential for developing a wholistic view of the human. In order to be experiential, creative, communicative, free, and expressive, one must be in the midst of a community that not only allows but encourages the development of these qualities and characteristics. Thus many young people are experimenting with or are on a quest for new forms of community. Communes are springing up everywhere—in rural areas, urban centers, and particularly in university communities.

Why these communes are being formed and what the recognized needs appear to be are difficult questions to answer. Some clues, however, may be discovered in an experiment that I conducted in study seminars on the emerging culture. As an introduction to the subject of revitalization of community, we engaged in a role-playing sequence. The three roles assigned were those of a mother, a father, and a son who had just completed his junior year in college. The parents anticipate that the son will spend this summer at home and receive some training in his father's business. In the course of the conversation the son is to inform his parents that he does not plan to live at home this summer but instead intends to establish a co-ed commune with some of his friends in the southwest. He wishes to experience this kind of living arrangement and has not yet decided whether or not he will return to college in the fall. In the role-playing sequence the son indicates the reasons why he no longer intends to live at home and wants to participate in this communal experience.

In the seminar I alternated between having parents and young people play their own roles and having two young people play the role of the parents and an older participant function as the college student. The fascinating thing about the results is that the reasons given for joining a commune were in substantial agreement regardless of who was playing the role. In other words, there was a kind of common awareness of the lack of community and those values for which one was reaching out in this experimental venture. The reasons often varied only in intensity and the order of concern.

In the seminar discussion of family relationships that followed, the most frequent complaint was that members of the family did not really listen to one another but presupposed the meanings and intentions of others in a given situation. Accompanying this inability authentically to listen and be sensitive was a concern for imposed expectations. The pattern of family life has become so structured and determined that it becomes almost impossible to take up a new stance or follow through on a particular interest without having that criticized and modified by the expectations of others, particularly by parents. There is, as a result, an insufficient respect and freedom for the diversity of viewpoints and authenticity of life-styles that differ radically. What the family unit lacks seems to be anything that approximates a common vision. Not only is there no agreement on the priorities, standards, and guidelines but no sufficient definition and discussion of these issues. In other words, there are no grounds for communication within a community that would provide an authentic and creative basis for support, criticisms, and renewal. The area in which one might hope to find the greatest resources for human understanding and creative renewal, the family, is found wanting.

The young have a frantic desire for an authentic, revitalized community, for sharing in another person's life, for the cocreation of each other's identity. "Together" is the word used to describe the special solidarity that undergirds the sense of community which the emerging culture wishes to nurture. The predominant theme of new communal life is "sharing." This involves money, possessions, clothes, cokes, pizza, and marijuana. But most of all, community is based on a shared vision of what it means to be human. It is constituted by shared values such as re-spect for individual uniqueness and privacy. The values that become operative are those of the peaceable kingdom which we discussed in the previous chapter in reference to the illuminating and transforming symbol of a new culture, peace.

There is, however, a special kind of shared value which pervades and enables this peaceful community to function. It is love. One might respond immediately that it is love which ties together the family unit. But the relationship we are talking about here has a dimension beyond conventional "family love" planted and cultivated only in terms of blood ties and loyalty contracts. The love that characterizes this form of communality, at least the form for which one strives, is not one that pursues the other's welfare in such a way that it seeks to possess him, protect him, and thus shape what he shall be.

The community rejects a self-possessing form of love, even if it claims to be based on the welfare of the other, for love in community, as sought by the emerging culture, is not understood to be that which is fully formed. Love is not individually given, but, rather, love is discovered and generated through a mutual sharing. Love is seen as a kind of gift in which the community is allowed to share and which ultimately liberates and enables others to become what they authentically are. However, a new consciousness about who we are as persons is essential for communities such as this to become a reality. To actualize this form of consciousness requires new symbols.

The notion of "communitarianism" articulated by Paul Goodman has spawned the preoccupation with participatory democracy and the concern of an increasing number of persons, young and old alike, to withdraw to a commune.[4] Some ask, "What leads to such an irresponsible abandonment of society?" Often the young forsake a society when it no longer commands respect or commitment. When this same society presses in upon you to cut your hair, control your language, contain your freedom, and possibly in Asia curtail your life—why not cop out? Or is "dropping out" really copping out? Perhaps it is only the refusal to make an "intelligent compromise" which will result in a teaching position, newspaper work, social service, or certain forms of political activism. Once you are merged with the society, you become indistinguishable from its mind-set and life-force except for a little extra hair here or there. The alternative, to organize a community of persons you love and respect or think you might grow to love, is perhaps a courageous and responsible act. If the purpose is to seek more viable models for community living where intrinsic human worth is recognized, enduring friendships are fostered, and creativity is encouraged, then this may involve what Buber calls, "pre-revolutionary structure-making."[5] However, to be fully responsible, to express a concern to humanize not only yourself but the society, you must attempt to transfer the model to the wider society when consciousness is transformed.

In order to experience transformation of consciousness, to achieve a new life-style, is it necessary to separate oneself physically from the dominant society? This is perhaps the most troublesome question in the discussion of a revitalization of community. Students are often perplexed and more than a little anxious about whether or not they really are a part of the emerging culture. Frequently a kind of defensiveness builds up when the subject is raised, because students usually have an allegiance to and agreement with the basic motifs, but have failed to implement the motifs with a new life-style. Thus the student is plagued with a kind of suspicion of hypocrisy for which the dominant society has been condemned. So the question remains, To commune or not to commune? Does liberation require absenting one's self from the society at least temporarily?

If one takes the uniqueness and intrinsic self-worth of the individual seriously, then it is impossible to answer that question finally or definitively. The imposition of a false consciousness, where one's life is determined by the values of the prevailing culture or subculture, is extraordinarily complex and pervasive. Therefore, if the existing society is debilitating to an extreme, if it so shapes and manipulates one's self-image that he is not free to realize his own potential, then indeed for some a separation or withdrawal from that society seems imperative and responsible.

However, it should be asserted that in order to achieve a transformation of consciousness, it is not necessary for everyone to separate himself physically from the dominant society. Were this necessary, the possibilities for authentic cultural revolution would be very slim indeed. Rather, I believe we are on the verge of a cultural revolution characterized by a gradual transformation of consciousness where people develop and incorporate new attitudes toward their roles in life and toward themselves. Let me cite two specific examples of groups whose members are forging a new sense of personal identity. They have been imprisoned in the stereotypes created by the present culture. In fact, their own members have often accepted and reinforced a false consciousness. Despite a move by some toward physical separation, the emphasis has been on internal transformation.

As the poster *White Man's World* so vividly depicts, the consciousness of the black man is constantly bombarded by what appears to him to be an alien imposition of another culture. Too often that culture predetermines the black man's

BELIEF AND THE COUNTER CULTURE

WHITE MAN'S WORLD

options regardless of his potential. So there is a demand either for separatism or a change in consciousness in order to rediscover the integrity of the black experience. According to the declaration of many blacks, separation is not imperative, but this move for many is both understandable and culturally persuasive. However, for an increasing number of blacks the declaration, "Black is beautiful!" reflects a dramatic change in self-understanding. The aim is not to accept or reject white values per se but rather to develop a notion of self and community authentic to the black experience.

It seems to me that this poster speaks to much more than just the black experience. It is applicable to any group or individual who feels as though an inauthentic environment and consciousness has been superimposed on him. Often he is not aware of the manipulative ordering of his experience and awareness. One may become suddenly conscious of this process and feel lied to and betrayed.

I have come recently to appreciate the similar predicament testified to by the movement called "Women's Liberation." The motifs articulated by those I know to be concerned with this movement are precisely those of a new consciousness. It is a consciousness for men as well as women that emphasizes a new way of relating to persons—not initially as men or women with certain prescribed roles, but rather as persons with unique, distinctive, and uncategorizable interests and capacities. The attempt here is to reconsider a humanity that denies the primary identification of a person in terms of sex.

Rather than be inauthentically incorporated into society's "accepted roles," many women strike out aggressively to forge new roles for themselves. Consequently, the concern expressed in Women's Liberation sometimes manifests itself in anger, defensiveness, and exaggera-

tion. But so does every form of cultural revolution with which I am acquainted. Insofar as many women object to predetermined role definitions such as wife, mother, and secretary, or to characteristics such as passivity, compliance, and gentleness, insofar as there is a primary impetus toward rehumanization, then Women's Liberation should be considered a part of the counter culture. It objects to the dehumanizing stereotypes of women in the dominant culture and seeks a transformation of consciousness for men and women alike.

A new life-style will be generated out of selective resistance to an imposed consciousness as well as a creative adaptation of events and experiences within one's present situation. Chapter II cites examples of young professionals who have transformed their work in order to make it more meaningful and more humane. A professional man or a housewife may transform his or her everyday activities by concentrating on more humane activities. He or she might enjoy regular periods of rest and revitalization, ignore the pressures of time, and emphasize the value of personal contacts either with business partners, members of the school or office car pool, with parking-lot attendants, custodians, and with the spouses and children of one's colleagues and competitors. I am persuaded that ways to implement new priorities and manifest the transformation of consciousness are discovered within the cultural context in which one finds himself. In fact, it is precisely this commitment to rehumanization which may in fact be the most vital component in bringing about the cultural revolution. Initially, this involves personal rather than structural change. This is obviously no simple matter and ought not to be naïvely or superficially contemplated. However, I am convinced that it is almost impossible for this transformation of consciousness to be achieved outside of a supportive community. Man by his very nature discovers who he is in relationship to others. He is fundamentally a creature of community, one who is shaped and affected by his culture not only by values and styles but inescapably by his language. It is, therefore, rare for a man to gain a transformation of consciousness in isolation without having the criticism, support, and renewal of a community. Man is what he is and what he shall be in relationship to others. Therefore, the emerging culture's fervent quest for the revitalization of community is not only appropriate but essential.

However, we have suggested that the nuclear family unit in its traditional form is often incapable or at least presently unwilling to provide the kind of communality that would make the process of rehumanization viable. Is the only option then to abandon the family structure in favor of an altogether new communal entity to be established in Arizona or in Chicago? I think not and, therefore, wish to propose two options in the form of models of new forms of communal living which in fact incorporate and depend on the family unit. They are not suggested as normative but only as additional models that merit consideration in the light of the crisis of communality. I present them because I think the question of whether it is necessary to absent oneself from society altogether or to remain a captive of the dominant consciousness is, in fact, a misleading question. Also, the decision to take up an altogether new form of communal life is enormous and demands exceptional conviction and more commitment than many of us are able to muster at this point of cultural uncertainty and confusion. The second model is suggested particularly because I think it is a practicable model that almost anyone convinced of the necessity of developing new forms of community could in fact adopt. Both are real models actually in operation, although some modification has been made for the purposes of this illustration.

Imagine, then, if you will, that someone invited you tomorrow to join a "family commune." Imagine first a situation where a group of families are dissatisfied with their present life-style. They feel unfulfilled and recognize their inability to relate to each other with the kind of freedom and fullness they desire. Therefore, they decide to go together and buy a large house or perhaps even an apartment house.

The group includes fathers with a variety of vocations—lawyers, medical doctors, teachers, laborers, insurance salesmen, postmen. There are obviously different salary ranges and a varied number of children involved in each family unit. They decide to move in together, to live in separate apartments, but to pool their incomes to live at a moderate level and to purchase beyond this advantages for culture, travel, and other necessities required by individual families. They take common meals together frequently and, in the case of this group, worship regularly together. The aim of their common life, however, is to build a community of support and renewal in which they can provide loving criticism and reflection upon their own priorities of time, money, and energy. Decisions are worked out in a corporate context concerning how the time and energy of the community will be invested, how finances will be allotted, and also what the roles and functions of the individual members might be.

A man is able to ask whether he really needs to work so hard for that new contract or that new appointment, a housewife considers whether she needs time away from her children in order to develop her own aesthetic or intellectual capacity. Parents and children alike ask how one deals with the educational process and a family life that allows for maturity and growth. Finally, the whole question of how children are raised becomes one of the most valuable topics of the family commune.

This commune provides a setting in which one may not only engage in and reflect upon his priorities but also find support and freedom to implement his decisions. This experiment has been functioning satisfactorily, although not without problems, of course, for a number of years and those within the community joyously attest to its success. They continually receive new members within the commune or encourage the creation of similar groups. Experience has released those within this community for new life-styles.

The second model is much more modest than this, but its implications are no less significant. This paradigm focuses around the experience of four families. They lived in the same geographical vicinity or within the same section of an urban area, yet were dissatisfied with the form of their communal life as well as with their individual existences. They felt that they had not maximized their potential and capabilities as individuals and that this failure was related to a lack of authentic community. Therefore they came together around a fireplace one night to discuss what they might begin to do about this concern which was authentic for their particular stage in life. The members of the group decided they were unwilling or unable to merge their family lives or to pool their incomes at this point. However, they did want to develop structures of communality that would place them in a significant relation and dialogue with each other on a regular basis. Therefore they decided they would commit themselves to meeting together for a minimum of eight hours every week. They would meet on a particular evening, beginning in the late afternoon and going on until midnight. They would be experimenting with new forms of community.

However, some shared visions and values undergirded this experiment. These were not precisely defined at the very outset, but they began to take shape in the process of this encounter. The first of these was to provide a greater variety of models of what it meant to be human—of what it meant to be sensitive, mature, responsible, and loving. The families felt that the models a husband and wife provided for their children were too limited. Therefore, they sought to expose not only each other's children to the model of their friends' humanity but also to have a closer encounter with these persons themselves. The initial stages of the family commune were, therefore, focused on the children, who ranged in age from one to fourteen years.

The opening hours of each experience were spent simply in play. The entire group would paint together, make sculpture, perform puppet shows, visit museums, fly kites, etc. But the object for the adults was to relate specifically to children other than their own. What was startling to the group was the image the adults initially presented to their friends' children. It was first of all that of "disciplinarian," a man or woman who said: "Turn down the stereo"; "Don't shoot the basketball in the living room"; and "Get off the grass—I just mowed and watered it." Or on the other hand, it was the paternalistic image of the mother or father who asked, "What did you do in school today?" and then didn't really listen to the answer. Also, mothers and fathers kept forgetting the names of the children's friends, to say nothing of their special interests and activities. In effect, parents were not really "clued in," were not really listening in the midst of these exchanges. So the play activity gave some opportunity for authentic conversation as did the common meal that they shared regularly together.

At the common meal, served each week in a different home, adults and children sought to sit

BELIEF AND THE COUNTER CULTURE

IT GETS LONELY

This print is available from Robert Hodgell, Box 46813, Pass-a-Grille Beach, Florida 33741

side by side instead of having the men sit in one area, the women in another, the older children at one, and the younger children at smaller tables to the side. The result was that after several weeks one father realized that children really do fascinating things in the fourth grade—he just never had bothered to listen before. Also, when it became apparent to the children that the adults in the group were genuinely interested in what they were doing, the conversation not only began to flow but the relationship to blossom.

The consequence of this rather simple effort was to develop types of communal relationships within what became "an extended family." Children who were simply too close and involved in a particular problem with their parents could go to one of the other parents in the group to get some perspective and then return to talk with their own parents. The younger children came to be free enough simply to go and play with other mothers or fathers. They attempted to share in the life-style of another family and by so doing to participate in a kind of incidental education for humanness. In return, parents found not only refreshing criticism but new insights from the children.

The group proceeded after the common meal to worship regularly together. The worship focused around a Christian Communion service in which every member of the group, including the younger children, shared in the service not only by songs and responses but by interpreting the Scripture or the theme for a particular evening. The service, therefore, had a kind of spontaneity, liveliness, and joy about it which made it one of the more significant services in which many members of the group shared. The service became a means of reflecting upon and embodying the shared visions and values of the group. It became the symbolic focus of their experience

together and, interestingly enough, was an event anxiously awaited by the children.

After joining together with some songs around a guitar or piano, there was a break while the younger children were taken home and put to bed. The adults and older children then continued their encounter with one another into the evening. The intent of these sessions was to develop a community of trust and of mutuality. Here one could begin to break down the barriers and images that he had built to protect himself not only from friends but also from family. This was an event in which one could begin to risk himself and to share commitments, hopes, and fears. A development of this trust did not come quickly, nor did it come without considerable pain. But it was nurtured to the extent that one could receive direct but loving criticism which necessitated a reevaluation of one's own priorities and life-style. This trust also facilitated a community of support; once one had reached a decision that seemed authentic for him, he had a community that liberated him to implement and employ that vision. But the community also freed him to abandon that vision or commitment if it was authentic for him to do so. The community, in other words, allowed one to recover his humanity. Specific questions were pursued concerning how one raised children; what the rights and privileges of children should be in the context of a family commune; how one apportions his financial resources; what one proposes to give his life and energy to and what he in fact did; whether one should strive for a new appointment, make a vocational or geographic move, or make a radical change in his own philosophy or life-style.

The result of this supportive, liberating, and humanizing community has been to allow some members of the family commune to have their lives transformed. They have adapted to this new phase of functioning within their vocation, new ways of relating within the nuclear family unit, and finally, new ways of expressing their own humanity and appreciating that of others.

If you were invited tomorrow to join a family commune, would you do it or would you not? And why or why not? In your reflections, choose your own model or modify either of these presented here. For many, the commune may not be structured along family lines at all, but rather lines of interest and shared values, particularly if a person does not operate within a family setting, or if that family setting is absolutely untenable for the nurturing of such a form of communality.

The employment of the questions or the models was simply to encourage you to take seriously the quest for a new form of community which is being urged by the emerging culture. You may wish to ask yourself whether the form of community and the relationships in which you presently share are adequate to sustain and develop your own humanity. Are there places where you can risk being authentically yourself and find acceptance, trust, and renewal in that risk? If you already have such a place, you are rare and fortunate indeed. If it is absent and yet you feel the need for it, what are the possibilities for discovering a revitalized community? If it is to take the form of a commune, what might its nature and impetus be?

We are painfully aware that many experiments in communal living are pathetic, as the movie *Alice's Restaurant* portrayed with poignancy. Why do such communes often fail? Perhaps it is because they lack a shared vision or a model that would enable one not only to believe in but to act on the assumption of intrinsic human worth, potential, and creativity. It is in relation to the need for a guide and stimulus to revitalize the notion of community and therefore to enable rehumanization that the notion of religion, or openness to transcendence, has a crucial role. Simply to reorganize or relocate a group of persons is no answer to the vacuity of community. The symbols that might provide an undergirding or the revivification of community must be experiential and intelligible. They will never be authentic symbols for the group until they are received as such. It has been suggested that illuminating and transforming symbols are the clue to what brings about a transformed consciousness. For the emerging culture, not only are these symbols and myths embodied by communities, but also they have a basically religious dimension. They are symbols of belief.

A goal of the emerging culture is the recovery of an authentic self in community. It is a quest to recover the human—a holy quest. A vision of the emerging culture proclaims that it is possible for man to exist as an authentic self, particularly a self in community, only on the basis of belief—a belief that serves to guide, shape, and orient the way in which one leads his life. But in what does the emerging culture believe? Faith must ultimately be in something that allows and engenders humanization. Faith is in a reality that enables man and his communities to be peaceable, loving, liberated, creative, and communal.

It is clear that the focus of this belief or faith is not in a machine, namely, in technocracy or the bureaucracy and structure that supports it. Man may use machines and techniques but he dare not believe in them and therefore come to trust and depend upon them. The present expansion of technology tends to minimize all the characteristics of the human that the emerging culture wishes to revive. When the machine dominates rather than serves, it can only dehumanize.

COMMUNITY AND THE TRANSCENDENT

Does the emerging culture believe, then, in man himself? Is the vision of the counter culture directed toward the liberated man, toward natural humanity freed of its cultural structures falsely imposed by a technocratic and bureaucratic society? Is this the new humanism that puts its faith and belief in man? No, I think not. Those who share in the emerging culture do not seem to anticipate that man will naturally and genuinely be loving, compassionate, sensitive, and sharing. Rather, these qualities are in the man who has been turned on, converted, and "gotten it all together." It is not the natural man, but rather the transformed man who makes the vision a reality.

What renews man? What transforms him? For the emerging culture to be humane requires an enabling force beyond the human. The belief of the emerging culture, the hope, and the optimism come out of an authentic openness to transcendence. This belief looks to a transcendent reality that will in fact make new both man and his community. There is a mysterious and awe-producing reality that in fact enables man to risk himself, to become more experiential, to manifest his creativity, to be able to touch and communicate with his brother, and finally, to manifest his desire for communality. Man seems incapable of doing this on his own, and yet miraculously and mysteriously it is happening.

The emerging culture is very religious indeed. This is evidenced in an openness to the Spirit which makes it impossible for one to predict and control what will occur. There is an openness to the authentically new that breaks in from the outside. But it is an openness to a transcendence that is fundamentally gracious. This transcendent reality is not in the first instance judgmental, but rather supportive, forgiving, and renewing. This faith is evident everywhere within the life-style of the emerging culture. The music of the culture symbolizes this in songs such as George Harrison's "My Sweet Lord" or the revival of "Amazing Grace."

Much art of the emerging culture, particularly that which is created communally, emphasizes in symbolic forms a transcendent power and on occasion declares it directly. This is exemplified in a delightful poster that focuses on joyous figures in an assortment of dress dancing across a brilliantly colored poster. This scene is surrounded by leafy green plants which could be taken to represent marijuana. The poster is entitled simply *God Grows His Own*. The poster declares something not only about plants but about a joyous new people that God is at work enabling and, as it were, growing.

Communes of every sort and variety focus around a central act of liturgy or ritual. Forms are diverse and sometimes bizarre, but in most instances they point to a transcendent power and reality beyond the individual and the community. The illuminating and transforming symbols of the new culture such as peace and love are understood primarily as gifts. They are not created but rather they are discovered and nurtured.

Those within the emerging culture, particularly the young, manifest an openness to transcendence and an awareness of the sense of the Spirit that challenges the institutionalized religious communities where the emphasis has been on formalized liturgies, controlled religious experience, and highly structured forms of community. The religious believer sits in worship praying openly, "Let God's spirit descend," but hopes like fury that it won't. For the presence of that Spirit would be uncontrollable and might bring about change and transformation. The emerging culture is not only open to the presence of that Spirit but actively seeks it and welcomes it. It is an encounter with the transcendent that brings about a transformation of consciousness.

The new symbol for a society with a changed consciousness, in counterdistinction to the cocktail party, will not be a rock festival, a fiesta, a be-in, or even a love-in. Rather, it could be a liturgy in which the meaning of life—all of life, in its sensuality and sacredness—will be thematized, symbolized, and celebrated. This would be a liturgy which lives up to its root meaning and becomes truly the work of a people as they dramatize and fantasize in order to receive a new vision of what it means to be human. This proposal may sound like the fantastic imaginings of a wild visionary without hope of actualization. And that would be true—without a radical transformation of the liturgy of life and of our consciousness. However, the new emerging culture declares that this is not beyond the capacity of Him whom people confess and call upon by many names. God, the mysterious, the transcendent, and even the Lord of Life.

It has been declared that the emerging culture in this country is very religious—but not necessarily Christian. Perhaps Charles A. Reich, one of the principal prophets of this emerging culture, points to an understanding of the message of the church that may make that fact intelligible. Reich declares: "Christianity asks men to give up power, aggression, and materialism for a promise of something better in another world, a world after death. . . . Christianity is just another form of giving up the present for some goal."[6] This is perhaps a justifiable critique of Christianity in its present cultural form. However, the emerging culture is reminding us that the Christian church, too, needs a transformation. It needs to recover its own visionary and apocalyptic character. It must reassert the symbolic words of its

Lord, "I came that you might have life and that you might have it more abundantly." The church must take seriously again a recovery of its own declaration, "And we shall have a new heaven and a new earth." And this does not commence only beyond the grave.

Many fundamental values of the emerging culture—transforming peace, liberating love, revitalized community, sacrificial concern—are embodiments of the Christian gospel. The young really believe what the church in its authentic moments proclaims about man and his world! Many in this emerging culture have also discovered what the church describes as the experience of grace—an enabling power to be healed, whole, free, loving, and thus a new creature. This transformation of consciousness occurs in community, and for some, including myself, this takes place within the revitalized community of Jesus Christ. The liberating promise of the gospel has been understood by the emerging culture in new forms. Now the church must be instructed by the witness of the counter culture which is both its heir and its prophet. The emerging culture is calling the Christian church and other religious institutions into confrontation. Its own religious dimension and sense of spirituality is calling into question the authenticity and lifestyle of religious institutions.

The young are beginning to call into question not only religious expression, but also our general Western myopia. Those persons who have lived at least briefly in non-Western cultures, mainly through the courtesy of the Peace Corps or the Military, and those who have studied the literature of the East, albeit in translation, have been confronted with new ways of understanding self, mind, and community environment. They have discovered in other cultures "emotional richness and maturity, powers of compassion, sensitivity, and endurance" that surpass what we experience in the West.[7] This is particularly true in nontechnological or so-called underdeveloped countries of the world. A taste of international culture has provided many with clues for a wider and richer concept of humanity. The future surely holds the promise and necessity of more intensive study in non-Western philosophy and religion. As a visiting theologian from India reminded me recently, many see the provincialism of the West as coinciding with an intellectual and cultural imperialism. We can no longer afford to deprive ourselves of the new insights and new approaches to old problems that a more intensive study of non-Western religions holds. The exclusivism of the Judeo-Christian tradition is being challenged particularly by the emerging culture.

"What theologian has influenced your generation most?" I had the naïveté to ask a seminary student recently. His answer was, "Alan Watts," an interpreter of Zen Buddhism in the West. Although this response may not necessarily be representative, it is significant. The counter culture has found itself turned on by Eastern religions and particularly by Zen Buddhism. Some of the interest appears faddish and superficial, but much is quite genuine and relatively well informed. Courses in comparative religion are enormously popular. Those within the church appear delighted that the young are interested in religion. The concerns of the neomystics are in contrast to the atheistic stance of previous cultural revolutions. However, what troubles these same religious people is the rejection by the counter culture of traditional ecclesiastical forms and formulas. It may be that this refusal cannot be accounted for simply as a desire to reject the Establishment religion. Rather, the young may well perceive that the contemporary expression of faith which has been characteristic of the church and synagogue in the West has had too narrow a view of reality, too constricted a consciousness. The Western believer has been too short on vision and too long on bureaucracy. The church has been too much oriented toward tools and institutions and not enough toward symbols and persons. In this way the emerging culture has called into question the relevance of our form of worship and of theologizing, specifically in its capacity to affect life-style.

This book has attempted to raise up for the sake of constructive confrontation and authentic communication the themes and motifs which characterize this cultural revolution. I have sought to interpret the vision of what it means to be human, fulfilled, joyous, and free as it has begun to be declared and lived out by the emerging life-style.

The themes of the counter culture which are actually developed depend, I believe, on radical openness to futurity and a God who encounters us in that sphere. Robert Neale notes in his work *In Praise Of Play* that play is the proper expression of religion. This insight guards against the tendency to take our discussion of predictions about matters of faith or culture with undue seriousness. Our reflection ought to be in Neale's sense playful and joyful, open to encounter and surprise. The posture of openness to surprise is vital to the religious consciousness and useful as preparation for any kind of encounter with the "children of change."

There is, I believe, a meaningful future for the self, the nation, and the culture. However, I hold this position only as an advocate of a necessary transformation of consciousness that results in a new life-style. Such a transformation holds the promise of a cultural revolution with the power of a symbolic illumination which is more experiential, emotional, mystical, communal, and above all visionary.

In Herb Gardner's play *A Thousand Clowns* the central figure is a man named Murray Burnes. He is compassionate, imaginative, sensitive, but also extraordinarily irascible. Murray is a rebel against conventional, structured society in the name of his own humanity and that of his nephew in whom he is trying to awaken the talents to observe the world and recognize the "phonies," to be creative, and to be spontaneous. Murray fears that his nephew will become a "list-maker," for whom everything is controlled and labeled, someone who loses his good eye for humor and humanity. Murray refuses to let the child become one of the "dead people" who have a gift and talent to "surrender and survive."

In one scene, Murray is confronted by a social worker intent on convincing him that he must adapt himself to the demands of the "real world." At one particularly frustrating point in the argument the sociologist cries out to Murray, "May God protect you from your vision!" Let us respond, "God forbid!" Our visions are our hope and our humanity. Our visions shall not only reshape but revitalize our future. Perhaps, indeed, they are the gift of God.

NOTES

I. Michael Novak(ed.), *American Philosophy and the Future* (Charles Scribner's Sons, 1968), p.10.

2. David Riesman, et al., *The Lonely Crowd: A Study of the Changing American Character* (Yale University Press, 1950).

3. Martin Buber, *Paths in Utopia* (Beacon Press, Inc., 1960), p.14.

4. Paul Goodman, *Drawing the Line* (Random House, Inc., 1962), pp. 97-111. Implications drawn by Theodore Roszak, *The Making of a Counter Culture* (Anchor Books, Doubleday & Company, Inc., 1969), p. 185.

5. Buber, *Paths*, pp. 44-45.

6. Charles A. Reich, *The Greening of America* (Random House, Inc., 1970), p. 346.

7. Herb Gardner, *A Thousand Clowns* (Random House, Inc., 1962), Act II.

A GUIDE
TO CONSTRUCTIVE CONFRONTATION

A Guide
to Constructive Confrontation

This Guide suggests a plan for conducting a study seminar with young people and adults that may assist in bridging the "generation gap" or "culture gap." In this seminar, persons of varying ages, who frequently have different visions, hopes, and expectations for themselves and their society, are invited to take an experiential trip through a constructive confrontation. The trip is a sustained encounter between persons of divergent viewpoints concerning crucial issues in their own life-style. The purpose of the encounter is not necessarily to bring the travelers into agreement, but rather into authentic communication with one another. The Guide was compiled as a consequence of my serving as a leader for twelve such constructive confrontations.

This Guide is based on the interpretive material on belief and the counter culture that precedes these pages, and an understanding of this material is essential for the would-be traveler. The Guide is a set of directions and information for travelers, and not a road map. It offers suggestions for:

The material contained here is to be construed as only suggestive. There are specific details for those who may find them useful. However, the participants know their own terrain and where they wish to go better than the author does. You must in fact experientially create your own journey if it is to be a meaningful and joyous sojourn.

I. GATHERING A TOUR GROUP

1. Who might be interested in a constructive confrontation?

The problems and the needs to which the package addresses itself seem to be evident in virtually every aspect of our culture. The crisis in communication, the so-called generation gap, concern for and uncertainty about proper priorities for the individual and the nation, a fear of violent revolution, substantial challenges to the educational system, dramatically increased drug usage, young people demanding to be heard and to participate, adults and particularly parents desperate to understand and to communicate—for whomever these issues are alive and by whomever these needs are felt, a *constructive* confrontation would be in order.

2. What organization or group might sponsor such an experience?

A confrontation could be a significant and exciting event to sponsor for many groups and organizations such as:

a church
a school PTA
a service club or civic organization
a professional group or labor union
a teen center or Boy Scout troop
or even a group of neighbors or friends
who are concerned about the problems mentioned

Wherever there is gathered a group of adults who have children or are concerned about the young, wherever there is a group of young people who have parents or older friends with whom they find difficulty in communicating and sharing, a constructive confrontation such as that described here may open up new avenues of communication, suggest new alternatives and insights, or simply allow them to achieve some clarity concerning the issues with which they are struggling.

There is one factor that is essential to a successful confrontation seminar. In each case it should begin from some sense of community, some specific relationship of the participants to each other. The confrontation experience is invariably more successful at meeting its aims when the members of the group are linked together by interest, organization, or other binding factors. It is not necessary that the participants know each other well or even be acquainted prior to the experience, but they should be able to identify a common relationship.

3. How many people should be included in the experience?

The optimum number seems to be between twenty and thirty. However, I have found it possible to conduct a seminar along these lines for as few as twelve and for as many as forty-five. During the experience the group will divide into much smaller parties. A group of twenty-four is large enough to allow for considerable diversity and freedom and yet small enough to permit people to become acquainted and engaged over a concentrated period. The total group selected should be divided equally between young people ranging from their mid-teens to early twenties and older participants running from their late twenties upward. The culture gap may not break down along these lines, but the division provides for direct conversation between two groups who have often assumed that they maintain different cultural perspectives.

In my experience it has been quite helpful to have families participate as units in the confrontation. This allows for persons who are frequently in conversation and conflict about the issues discussed to encounter each other and to have a basis upon which to apply almost immediately any results of the seminar.

Obviously, the greater diversity that can be incorporated into the group the better. Therefore, it has been a very beneficial procedure for the agency or persons sponsoring the event to issue personal invitations to individuals and families to participate in this experience. This allows for some selection of those who have different perspectives on cultural issues, and the personal invitations also tend to increase a sense of commitment to the experience.

In writing your invitation, you might do these things:

1. Give participants a clear idea about what they will be involved in.

2. Indicate that responsibility and commitment to carry through the entire venture is essential. (It is imperative that a participant understand that he is expected to be involved in the total experience insofar as that is possible.)

3. Briefly outline the major events that will occupy the day or the series of sessions.

A sample invitation is not provided here, because it is important that the invitation for each group be designed to focus specifically on the issues most relevant for its particular requirements.

You may wish to give this experience a name other than "Constructive Confrontation" for the purposes of publicity, invitations, and interpretation. For example, you might describe it as a study seminar and entitle it "Belief and the Counter Culture," "Belief and the Youth Culture," or "A Constructive Confrontation Between the Establishment and the Dissenters."

II. USING THE RESOURCES

The total contents of this package should be considered as resource material for the constructive confrontation. This includes:

written interpretive material
reproductions of posters and prints
music

simulation game
role-playing sequence
an art project

Supplementary resource materials recommended for use include suggestions for a film, additional recordings, and some full-sized posters. The additional material is optional and not required.

There are different ways in which the interpretive materials, records, and prints in this package might be employed creatively as a resource for such an experiential encounter. The total package might be a preparatory resource which each participant in the seminar would be encouraged to read and experience prior to the seminar. In this way the material would be employed as a catalyst to broaden horizons and pinpoint issues of controversy or agreement. Another approach would be for the leader and perhaps only a couple of other participants to be knowledgeable concerning the resources and then suggest that the group as a whole encounter the resources in the process of the confrontation itself. This method emphasizes the spontaneity of the group and employs their natural responses, insights, and biases as catalytic agents rather than the interpretive material. The leader could then suggest using this book as follow-up material, since particular issues raised in the confrontation are dealt with at greater length and may provide the foundation for continued discussion or concrete activities aimed at bridging the culture gap. The sponsor could encourage every participant to secure his own package, or he might give one to each person at the conclusion of the seminar. (The price could be included in the registration fee.)

Any of these suggested methods may be modified, or they can readily be combined. The point is that the leader should use the resources as multisensory catalysts which induce the participants to engage in authentic dialogue and therefore constructive confrontation. It should be emphasized again that the focus of the project is to stimulate just such a confrontation. To consider the material only an intriguing or questionable thesis about a cultural revolution, and therefore not to experiment with the ideas in a communal context, is to leave the project stillborn.

III. SELECTING A COMPETENT LEADER

The leader of this constructive confrontation obviously plays a crucial role. It is imperative to stress from the very beginning that the leader should see himself as an enabler and a facilitator of the confrontation. His role is not that of an instructor, gadfly, or monitor of the cultural crisis. The leader you select should not hold an authoritarian position within the organization or group, nor should he be a person with an authoritarian stance or personality. Therefore, it is generally not advisable to select as the group leader the president of a civic club or PTA, or the staff member of an organization, i.e., the pastor or executive secretary. By the nature of their office or role these persons often inhibit free and open criticism and dialogue among the participants in the group. Usually it is wise to ask a person who is outside the group to function as the leader for the constructive confrontation. However, if it is necessary to choose a leader from your group, he should be someone who enjoys or is likely to receive wide acceptance throughout the group and tends to liberate people to respond freely and critically in his presence.

The leader need not necessarily be an individual who is experientially or cognitively knowledgeable about the motifs of the emerging culture. However, he should be a person who has some acquaintance with the counter culture and some openness to the kinds of new positions advocated. The leader's ability to listen, his capacity as an enabler of participation, conflict, and reconciliation, and his skill in keeping the group alive and moving should be the determinative factors in selecting him.

IV. SELECTING THE LOCATION AND GATHERING EQUIPMENT

1. Where to meet.

A variety of locations is acceptable. The primary need is for a relatively large and comfortable room that will provide adequate space in which everyone can stretch and expand. The area needs to be big enough to allow small groups to get together in various parts of the room where they will not interrupt each other. A facility that has several smaller rooms, or at least one adjoining room, is very useful. An informal lounge-type room equipped with reasonably comfortable chairs or a rug on the floor is helpful. It is particularly advantageous to select a location that has:

a. Walls or blackboards on which to display prints and posters.

b. Enough space for the group to create its own environment by rearranging the chairs, lying on the floor, or gathering in small groups as particular parts of the seminar suggest.

c. Sufficient privacy to prevent interruption by other groups or individuals.

A possible location might be a church parlor, a student lounge, a large classroom, or even a gymnasium or recreation room. However, if those attending are creative and flexible, almost any informal setting will do.

2. What equipment to gather.

The equipment for the seminar will vary according to the particular options that are selected and the resources employed. The basic equipment is readily obtainable and reasonably inexpensive. Items such as record players or a film projector can often be acquired on loan from a school or church or rented for a modest fee.

The dominant culture has instructed us that even a small financial investment tends to entice and focus our interest. Therefore, it is often helpful to charge each participant, including the young people, a small fee. This covers expenses such as acquisition of equipment, a copy of *BELIEF AND THE COUNTER CULTURE* for each participant, coffee break and food supplies, or an honorarium for an outside leader. It is also a means of enhancing an individual's commitment to the seminar itself.

Here is a suggested equipment checklist for your reference and aid:

CONSTRUCTIVE CONFRONTATION SUGGESTED EQUIPMENT CHECKLIST

- Name tags—the stick-on variety—and Magic Markers.
- Two record players capable of playing 33 1/3 speed.
- Film. *Why Man Creates* is suggested.

To order for a rental fee of $10 to $15:

Write   (1)   Pyramid Films, Box 1048, Santa Monica, Calif. 90406;

or   (2)   Learning Resources Service, Southern Illinois University, Carbondale, Ill. 62901;

or   (3).   inquire at the film library of any large public or university library.

- 16mm. film projector.

Note: (1)   If a film is to be shown, it must be ordered at least two weeks in advance.
    (2)   Be sure to preview the film before you plan to use it with the group.
    (3)   Have the screen and projector set up in advance and have a qualified person to run the projector.

- A chalkboard, chalk, and eraser.
- A large bulletin board or some area where a series of posters may be displayed; thumbtacks or masking tape.

Note:
(1) If full-sized posters are to be hung, purchase or order them in advance.
(2) Posters can be obtained by writing to the addresses indicated with the reproductions of the posters in this book. The cost of each poster will range from $1.50 to $3.00. A list of additional posters is also available from the firms noted.
(3) You might also ask the young people to bring their favorite posters.

Copies of the prints may be ordered directly from Robert Hodgell, Box 46813, Pass-A-Grille Beach, Fla. 33741. These signed originals on rice paper cost from $15 to $25.

- Pencils and paper.
- Art supplies.

a. Very large sheets of sturdy white paper, such as several commercial brands of shelf paper or a roll of white butcher paper.
b. Finger paint. Buy commercially prepared finger paint or use this recipe to make your own:

You need: wheat flour   several small bowls
              cold water   one large bowl
              food color or tempera paint

Put water into large bowl *first*. Stir in wheat flour until desired consistency. Stir vigorously for a couple of minutes to avoid lumps. Divide paste and add coloring.

c. Smocks, or ask participants to bring old long-sleeved shirts.

3. What food preparations to make.

Depending upon the specific schedule selected by your group, appropriate arrangements for meals and coffee breaks should be made in advance. For example, if the seminar will be held all in one day, you would include two coffee breaks, lunch, and/or supper. Box lunches, pot-luck, or cafeteria-style service is suggested for your meals. The fewer responsibilities the group participants have in these preparations, the better.

V. DEVISING A WORKABLE SCHEDULE

The precise schedule must be determined, of course, by the nature of the group and its own particular circumstances. Whatever schedule is devised should be communicated clearly to the group as a whole and changed only with their consent in the form of a corporate decision. Flexibility by the leader and the group are essential to adapt to your own location.

Possible schedules include a Retreat, a Series of Separate Seminars, and a One-Day Seminar.

Retreat

Many people prefer a retreat setting so that members of the group are not tempted to wander off during the day or get engaged with nonseminar participants during the experience. Under retreat conditions people have the opportunity to become acquainted with each other more slowly and naturally. They become involved in common tasks and activities together, such as taking meals and enjoying recreation. The themes and motifs of the particular sessions can then be expanded in informal conversations. Issues of conflict can be followed out personally and directly, yet the group maintains an identity of its own. However, the lengthy retreat method is often not practical for many groups because of the time commitment and the possible expense.

Series of Separate Seminars

Another option is to conduct a series of separate sessions that would be either one hour or one and a half hours in length. The series could number five, six, seven, or eight seminar sessions. This method allows the resource material to be employed gradually and progressively, with a section of the material being assigned for each week.

The confrontation experience is divided into eight one-hour sessions. Some of these sessions could be combined to fit into a schedule of five, six, or seven separate seminars.

In five seminars or meeting times, you might combine the sessions as follows:

Sessions One and Two
Session Three
Session Four
Session Five
Sessions Six, Seven, and Eight

In six seminars, combine:
Sessions One and Two
Session Three
Session Four
Session Five
Session Six
Sessions Seven and Eight

The method of separate seminars is less concentrated and intense and is very practical for those organizations oriented around continued programs for study seminars or discussion groups. However, it endangers continuity and totality of impact.

One-Day Seminar

The one-day seminar running from approximately 8 A.M. to 6 P.M. is the most feasible and economical plan so far developed. This is clearly a concentrated and somewhat exhausting experience. I have discovered that the intensity and the length of the session tend to encourage a sense of community and commitment. It allows enough time for some conflicts to be worked through emotively as well as cognitively, for solutions to be reached, and for patterns of developing relationships to emerge. The intensity and length have the additional advantage of tending to break down the rather superficial barriers among individuals.

Another definite asset in the possibility of having the total experience conducted in one block of time, probably on a Saturday or a Sunday, is that this involves only one meal, which can be handled either on a box-lunch or potluck basis. Those who may wish to attend as families can make baby-sitting arrangements for their younger children as a group. Finally, this plan tends to guarantee a continuity of experience for the participants.

The following is a suggested basic schedule for a one-day confrontation indicating how the eight sessions might be spaced. It is not necessary to maintain a set schedule. Rather, allow some sessions to run longer if they are going well, and cut others short if interest appears to lag. The schedule is only a guideline. The leader must function as a tour guide and not a traffic cop. The success of the seminar in terms of expanded awareness is the responsibility of the whole group and not his alone. The leader must "hang loose," be sensitive to where the group is, and suggest transitions at appropriate times.

SUGGESTED ONE-DAY SCHEDULE

Session One.   *Introduction—Preparation for Confrontation*
(8:30-9:30 A.M.)
A. Getting acquainted—What does it mean to be human?
B. What is a cultural revolution?

Session Two.   *Priority of Experience*
(9:30-10:30 A.M.)
A. Mini-simulation game
B. Reflection upon priorities and decision-making
Coffee Break (Rest Period)   (10:30-10:45 A.M.)

Session Three.	*Recovery of Mystery and Restoration of Creativity*	
		(10:45-12:00 A.M.)
	A. Use of music of the emerging culture, or film *Why Man Creates*	
	B. Creativity and mystery for us	
Lunch		(12:00-1:00 P.M.)
Session Four.	*Communication and New Symbols*	
		(1:00-2:00 P.M.)
	A. Use of poster-art and prints	
	B. Discovering and interpreting symbols	
Session Five.	*Art Project—A Form of Symbolic Expression*	
		(2:00-3:00 P.M.)
	A. Communal finger-painting and music	
	B. What do our symbols say?	
Session Six.	*Revitalization of Community*	
		(3:00-4:00 P.M.)
	A. Role-playing about communes	
	B. What form of community?	
Coffee Break		(4:00-4:30 P.M.)
Session Seven.	*Openness to Transcendence and the Future*	
		(4:30-5:30 P.M.)
	A. Belief in what?	
	B. Plans for the future	
Session Eight.	*Evaluating and Concluding the Event*	(5:30-6:00 P.M.)

VI. PROCEEDING THROUGH THE SESSIONS

With a general outline of the eight sessions in mind, consider now specific suggestions for each session.

Session One. Introduction—
Preparation for Confrontation

It is important to encourage a prompt arrival by all participants. The leader should greet each person on his arrival and begin informal introductions. Encourage the participants not to di-

vide along age lines for warm-up conversations. The initial process is facilitated by asking each participant to make out his own name tag as he comes in, employing the stick-on variety if possible. The leader might request that each participant print his first name only, using large clear letters.

As soon as almost all participants have arrived, gather the group into a large circle or any arrangement that allows those present to see one another. The leader may then make some informal remarks concerning the aim and expectations of the day. If a majority of the participants have had an opportunity to read this book, the leader may wish only to remind them of certain primary goals. If they have not, he can be somewhat more precise, drawing his material from the first two chapters.

The leader should take no more than ten minutes for these remarks and should proceed in an informal manner, emphasizing his role as a participant in the day's activities and not as an instructor. Therefore, it is useful for the leader to be seated with the group in a circle instead of speaking from behind a lectern or a table. He must set the model for informality and receptivity.

In his introductory remarks the leader might wish to stress the following:

1. *Informality*. Request the use of first names only. This is a way to eliminate a rather superficial barrier of titles that sometimes separates us either in an authoritarian or a paternalistic way.

2. *Honesty*. It is essential for everyone to be as frank and direct with others as possible in discussing priorities, concerns, and visions. This is not a seminar to "psyche out" the young, but everyone's priorities are up for grabs. Sharing is crucial.

3. Emphasize the present *crisis in communication*. Note that some interpreters suggest that we are on the verge of a cultural revolution which demands the reconsideration of our own personal priorities and life-styles. Make use of illustrations of the communication gap or the coming cultural revolution drawn either from the interpretive material or from actual situations.

4. *Belief*. Stress the importance of belief and commitment, if only implicit, as integrating and directing one's own life-style. The computer story from Chapter II might serve as an illustration or reminder here.

Proceed by asking each participant to introduce himself briefly to the group. In so doing, he is to answer two questions:

1. What are the real reasons why he came to the seminar?

Perhaps the organizer "twisted his arm," or his son or daughter or another young person pressured him into participation, or a parent coerced a young person into joining the seminar. Encourage people to express clearly their expectations concerning the experience and the reason for their interest in this particular encounter.

2. What *one* characteristic would introduce the participant to the group?

He might consider the many things that would identify him, what he thinks is most important about who he is as a person. This is a difficult question, and people may need to be gently prodded really to answer it. Try to move beyond the superficial identification of people by their occupation, age, or cultural role. The leader's own sense of humor can help people to feel comfortable in this initial discussion and thus avoid defensiveness on the part of some people for the rest of the day. The leader might indicate that it is perfectly acceptable, for instance, not to know what *one* thing characterizes a person. Or he might suggest that some people's responses may be in terms of a present consuming interest or even a hang-up. Encourage everyone to speak briefly and keep the conversation flowing. The leader should be sure to provide a similar introduction for himself.

Continue by suggesting that each participant now try to name the characteristic that identified their fellow participants. In the pause that invariably follows, some will probably express consternation and anxiety, often jokingly, about their inability to do what is suggested. The leader might say that he would be interested in following through with a suggestion made, but will not do so. Rather, he would employ the experience to make the point that people ordinarily are so preoccupied with what they are going to say about themselves that they fail really to listen and remember what another participant says about himself. The leader should help the group to observe that it is just this facility to listen and respond that the seminar hopes to enhance. One must learn to hear the questions and concerns that stand behind the expressed statement of a seminar participant.

The second major observation that may be made about the introductory process is that each one has been asked to identify what characterizes him. This is another way of expressing the question at the root of the emerging culture, What does it mean to be human? The leader might encourage the group to express opinions regarding what not only does, but should, identify us as persons and as members of a community. (Surely not the things that we normally indicate in a formal introduction.) Explain that the stages of the confrontation will focus on certain themes and motifs concerning what it means to be human.

Finally, the leader may wish to remind the group that one of the major intentions of the day is for everyone to have a joyous experience— to have fun. Explain briefly some of the activities of the day that may involve a simulation game, a movie, poster art, contemporary music, role-playing and finger-painting. Move then directly into the second stage by introducing a simulation game as a way in which one may hope to enjoy the experience.

Session Two. Priority of Experience
The leader might begin by asking how many have participated in a simulation game before. Probably relatively few have, and therefore some brief definition of a simulation game is needed.

1. It should be noted that this is a mini-simulation game in which a particular concrete situation will be described. The participants will be asked to take on certain roles in order to project themselves into this situation.

2. Some will be asked to simulate an experience in which they will be twenty or thirty years younger or older then they are at present.

3. Participants should be cautioned, however, against creating stereotyped roles. Don't pretend to be someone entirely different from what you are. Simply project yourself into that situation at a particular age. Make an attempt to empathize and share imaginatively with those who may have a different cultural perspective.

4. The situation, like life, will change as new information is introduced by the gamekeeper (the leader).

5. The participant needs to make decisions on the basis of the information that is before him. That information, however, can be expanded or modified, and one must be flexible enough to deal with his feelings and emotions in decision-making processes such as these.

The leader may wish to clarify some questions, but should not let the group get hung up on defining all the rules. Encourage people simply to experience the game, to work at it, and enjoy it.

Step 1
The leader should now set the situation which might be shaped to fit the particular group sponsoring the seminar. The group members will be

asked to simulate particular roles within the life of that community or organization to which the members belong. In the game parents and young people will try to persuade a decision-making body to accept their suggestions on three controversial issues.

Step 2

Ask the group to count off by threes, or somehow divide themselves into three relatively equal groups. Counting off is probably the quickest and simplest, but the leader may need to do some shifting to make sure that there is a general balance of young people and adults in each given section.

The "ones" are to constitute the decision-making body of the particular organization. This might be the officers, the official board, the executive committee, the vestry, etc. Out of this group select one person to be the moderator or presiding officer. It should be someone who is articulate and manifests a degree of self-confidence, but who would not ordinarily be placed in such a position. In many instances this might be a young person or a woman.

The "twos" are to constitute a special committee of parents within this particular organization. Hypothetically, the age of this group runs from thirty to sixty. The members may select their own roles within that range as long as some diversity is maintained.

The "threes" are to constitute a body of young people who are officially or unofficially members of the simulated group. In a church situation they may be actual participating members. However, in a civic club or PTA, they may be the sons and daughters of those who are members of the organization.

Step 3

When each participant understands his role, explain that the parents and the young people will be presenting reports to the decision-making body on three controversial issues within the community. Recall that the goal of the game is for each group to try to persuade the decision-making body to adopt its proposals for a public stand on the issues. This will be a statement either before their membership or before the community at large. Each group may influence the decision-making body by any appropriate means—by the persuasive nature of their report, or by other means of extending their influence, as determined by each group. The final decision will be made as to which positions are adopted on the basis of vote. The votes are distributed as follows:

The decision-making body, or "the board" .... 15 votes
The parents committee .... 10 votes
The young peoples' committee .... ½ vote
(There will no doubt be some controversy over this final allotment. The leader may ask whether this is not in fact a little generous for the influence that young people usually have in particular organizations.)

The three issues and problems to be considered are:

1. A decision is needed concerning the dress code in the public high school. This involves clothing, hairstyle, and foot covering. Assume that there has been a controversy in your community over a male high school student who appeared in class without shoes or shirt. The committee should discuss whether there should be a code at all and what form it might take. A second part of this question might involve the question of dress at the meetings of this particular organization and whether any guidelines, formal or informal, should be introduced.

2. Action is being considered by an outside institution to establish a research center to study the use, effect, and implications of marijuana

and psychedelic drugs. The center will be established with competent leadership. It will employ volunteers from the community, who will be carefully screened and tested under controlled and guided circumstances. The group is being asked whether it would support the establishment of such a research center in its local community.

3. The board of education has given notice that it is considering introducing into the high school curriculum the following year an elective course for seniors on the sociological and political implications of revolution. The instructor for the course will be a recent graduate of a regional university that has been involved in controversial student activities and disruptions. (The leader should supply the name of a particular institution such as Columbia, Northwestern, the University of California at Berkeley, for example.) The course will also involve field work, although that is presently undefined.

Step 4

The leader should then assign to each group an area in which to carry on their discussion. Announce that the time allowed will be approximately thirty minutes to develop their positions on all three issues. Each group should appoint a recorder and a spokesman.

The leader may move from group to group—not to interfere with the discussion, but to encourage the group to make decisions and to express their personal feelings on the issues at hand. Depending on the circumstances and how much the group is enjoying the game, the leader may want to extend the amount of time allotted. But time should be kept relatively short in order to pressure the groups to get to the point and concentrate on the issues developed.

Step 5

At the end of the allotted time the leader should reconvene the groups and ask the appointed moderator to conduct the meeting. The problems should be considered in order, allowing for a report from the young people and from the adults, and questions and responses from the board. The leader should encourage strong expression and feelings of conflict to develop. On occasion he may need to take the proposal of one of the two groups and shape it into a brief declaratory statement.

Suggestions for the leader: He should encourage the group to get at the basic questions that underlie each particular issue. Incorporated in the *first* issue, for instance, is the relationship of any code or standard to the freedom of an individual to determine his own dress. The further consideration is that if dress is a matter of the authenticity and self-expression of the individual, does this guideline also apply to morals and political and cultural stances? On this first issue the leader would introduce no additional information, but would help to keep the conversation lively. To bring the discussion to a conclusion he would ask the respective groups to caucus and then cast their votes. Allow them to split their vote among the individuals within the group. The results should then be tallied and announced with as little delay as possible.

On the *second* issue, after there has been general discussion of the reports and responses, and the group is preparing to come to a vote, the leader could introduce some added information that has just come to light. For example, it appears that the center will be founded and established by an educational foundation such as the Ford or Carnegie Foundations. Report that the "competent leadership" promised has been announced to be three former associates of Dr. Timothy Leary. They had continued their research on the use of drugs after Dr. Leary left the association. This research was conducted in another state that subsequently discouraged its continuation because it was rumored that the research was encouraging the use of marijuana and psychedelic drugs. The three men are academically competent: one has a doctorate in biochemistry, one has an M.D. with specialized training in the use of drugs, and the third is a practicing psychiatrist. The results of their former research had neither been completed nor published, but there was a public furor about their presence.

On the basis of this added information, ask the particular groups to caucus and to vote. It may be interesting to see to what degree the stereotypes associated with certain public figures and public issues influence the decision of the group. Is there a prior bias toward either the harmful effects or the neutral implications of the use of drugs which would cause presuppositions about how the research will turn out? Finally, attempt to encourage the group to deal with the question of why one would seek the extended experimentation with drugs in their own community.

On the *third* issue, the leader might again introduce additional information after the specific reports have been received and briefly discussed. Prior to caucusing for the vote, the leader should suggest that additional information has come to light concerning the nature of the elective. The instructor selected for the course has no particular bias either for or against revolutionary activity. He has suggested, however, that he intends to have a series of guests in the course who will present vividly the attitudes of diverse groups within the culture on the issues of revolution. These may include the SDS, the Black Panthers, a representative of the police department, an economist, a representative of Moral Re-Armament, and perhaps a socially active minister. The fieldwork will not involve actually initiating a revolution; it will attempt to acquaint the class with procedures that are involved both in organizing a revolution and in controlling revolutionary activities. In other words, a number of options and issues will be examined that will involve exposure to enthusiastic advocates of these positions. Then ask the groups to caucus before the final vote.

Step 6
Finally, draw the group together and ask them to reflect on the experience they have just had. Comment that they have engaged in an illustration of the first motif of the emerging culture, emphasis on the priority of experience and subjective involvement. Ideas from Chapter III of the interpretive material might be integrated into this discussion.

Encourage the group to identify specific problems as well as feelings that arose during the encounter. Were the issues discussed realistic? Did participants feel that others in the group were being honest and frank about their opinions, or were they in fact fostering "stereotypes"? How did the young people and the adults feel about the proportionate power allotted to the youth committee? Finally, out of this simulated experience what particular problems might the sponsoring organization want to focus on in terms of deriving more information, considering a wider range of options, and perhaps interpreting controversial issues to its own membership or the community?

Suggestions for the leader: He should feel free to change or modify any of these suggestions in order to substitute particular problems that are emerging within the organization or community. The aim is to introduce some active dialogue on issues that are pushing in the direction of cultural transformation. The leader should feel free to allow the game to carry on longer than an hour if people are actively involved and getting at fundamental issues. He may not find it necessary to go through all three problems, but only one or two if useful interaction is developing.

The leader may find it helpful to the participants to begin to list on a large chalkboard the basic themes of the counter culture. Follow this procedure throughout the day, adding each motif as it is considered. The themes are:

1. Priority of experience and subjective involvement
2. Recovery of mystery and restoration of creativity
3. Concern for communication and the symbolic dimension
4. Revitalization of community and openness to transcendence

Session Three. Recovery of Mystery and Restoration of Creativity

"Creativity" and "mystery" are words that we talk about a lot and experience very rarely. Therefore, this stage of the trip could focus on one of two forms of creative media—music or film.

Music

The first option is to utilize at this point the recordings by Kathy Gregory and other contemporary music which is applicable. Several additional records and albums have been recommended in Chapter IV. Kathy's songs often point to a sense of mystery and are examples of the creativity characteristic of the emerging culture.

1. Session Three might begin simply by allowing the group to listen to various forms of music that have been so important for the emerging culture. This should be done first without providing the words or libretto for any of the songs or operettas that might be employed. Encourage the participants to experience the music as a whole without systematically analyzing the lyrics, tune, instruments, etc.

2. The leader might then begin discussion on the nature and significance of contemporary music, focusing on rock music and the country ballad. Participants should be encouraged to express their questions, fascination, or frustration with these forms of music. Ask the participants how they respond to:

the volume,
the manner in which the lyrics are communicated,
the content of the lyrics.

The members of the group might explore the reasons why they appreciate the music, are moved by it, or are disturbed by it. The listeners might consider whether this music:

is genuinely creative or only superficial,
directs one's attention and senses toward mystery or is simply distracting,
confronts one as a total experience or functions as meaningless noise.

This is a discussion where the young people might provide some extraordinary insights and interpretations for those participants less familiar with this style of music.

3. The leader may want to be conscious of the interpretive reasons suggested for the form this music has taken as noted in Chapter IV and offer them for discussion. It might be useful to select a couple of songs and examine their lyrics with some care. This could be done with any of Kathy Gregory's songs. For this purpose, the lyrics to those songs can be found at the end of the Guide.

Sample questions that may stimulate discussion on some of Kathy's songs are:

"Prepared for Killing"
How is the question of self-defense viewed here?
Are symbolic attitudes of our society exposed here?

Is the social comment provocative or simplistic?

"After Cambodia"
What stance is taken toward violence?
Is this song an indication of the cultural revolution?
How prominent or authentic is the symbol of peace?

"Celebration"
What belief is proclaimed here if any?
What vision of life is behind the celebrative stance?

The leader might also select Arlo Guthrie's "Alice's Restaurant Massacree"; Leonard Cohen's "Suzanne"; or the song of Mary Magdalene, "I Don't Know How to Love Him," from the rock opera *Jesus Christ Superstar*. Appropriate questions could be posed by the leader.

Film

The leader may decide that he can employ the music more advantageously in the fourth session, which deals with communication. In this case he could choose the second option for Session Three and suggest that the group enjoy the extraordinary film *Why Man Creates*. It is one of the more creative and suggestive films that the author has encountered and is highly recommended as a stimulus for the discussion of creativity. If the morning session has gone much beyond its suggested schedule, this film can be shown effectively during the noon meal, particularly if people have brought a box lunch.

If the film is to be used, the leader may wish to make a few very brief comments by way of introduction, saying that the recovery of mystery and restoration of creativity are two important motifs in the cultural revolution.

After the film has been shown, ask the group what kinds of feelings they had as a result of watching it. Encourage people simply to express themselves at this point and share general reactions to the film. It is usually fascinating to note how difficult it is for us to discuss an emotional rather than an intellectual reaction. Recall that one of the concerns of the emerging culture is that we have become too inhibited to express our feelings freely and honestly.

After a few minutes of general discussion, follow up what appear to be pertinent issues in which the participants are interested. The leader might ask the viewers to close their eyes for a few minutes and think about the film. When a half a minute or so has elapsed, ask the group what image from the film first came into their minds when they began to reflect upon it. Why do they think that image was important to them?

At this point the leader may continue with the discussion, letting the participants follow up and respond to each other's suggestions. The interpretive material included in Chapter IV may be useful in highlighting certain points in the discussion.

Questions and issues that the leader may want to keep in mind in discussing the film are:

1. What was the judgment made about the progress of civilization as evidenced in the edifice?

2. What was the ultimate criterion offered by society concerning creativity in the segment dealing with the artist's effort to create with his blocks?

3. What was the attitude represented toward time in the sequence involving the four scientists?

4. What did the parable about the Ping-Pong

ball have to say about creativity and the reaction to it within our society? Did you identify with the Ping-Pong ball, and if so, why?

5. What did the film seem to be saying about why man creates? Did it appear that creativity is an important element in what it means to be human?

6. How do you manifest your own concern for creativity and the mysterious? How does the community support you in this effort?

Suggestions for the leader: In this third session in utilizing either music or the film a conscious attempt ought to be made to avoid being too controlled, too much "under wraps." The leader should allow the session to grow creatively and spontaneously, focusing on the challenge of creativity and mystery and the way in which they affect the members of the seminar.

Session Four. Communication and New Symbols
The emerging culture is not simply an ear-oriented phenomenon. Rather, visual images and the phenomena of touch are thought to be as important if not more important than what one hears. In this concern for communication, or "rapping," there is a new sensitivity to the role that symbols and myths play in communication. Suggest to the group that they are going to have the opportunity to respond to and experience two of the more popular forms of symbolic communication, poster art and music.

There are several ways in which the leader might utilize the posters and prints. The initial approach in this session depends on what materials the leader has available.

1. If each participant has a copy of *BELIEF AND THE COUNTER CULTURE*, he can easily study the fourteen posters and prints spaced throughout the book.

2. Should a number of full-sized posters be available, these can be placed throughout the room by the participants, using either masking tape or thumbtacks. Suggestions for acquiring posters and prints are noted on the equipment checklist, p. 107.

3. For wider variety, the leader could utilize in addition to the posters and prints in this book any full-sized posters he can assemble. However, there is not necessity for acquiring additional material, since the package resources are intended to be adequate. Additions do tend to provide variety and enhance the experience.

A workable procedure for studying the posters is to request the members of the group either to study the book illustrations or to wander around the room viewing the posters on display. Ask each person to identify two particular posters: first, the poster that most "turns him off," repels him, or aggravates him; second, the poster that speaks to him most adequately (not necessarily the one he likes best, although that might also be the one) and carries for him the greatest impact. Encourage the group to thumb slowly through the book or to circle the room in a leisurely way to enjoy the experience, chatting with one another and reflecting about the posters and the music.

This might be a good time to utilize some additional folk or rock music, such as the rock operas *Tommy*, by The Who, and *Jesus Christ Superstar*, or George Harrison's album *All Things Must Pass*.

After ten or fifteen minutes, ask each member in the seminar either to mark the page in his book or go and stand beside the poster on display which most repels him. When the group is ready, ask people to point out which poster they have chosen and tell why they feel as they do. If other members of the group have a different interpretation of the poster, they should feel free to express it.

Now ask each participant to indicate the poster that he felt was most significant for him. Once again, ask the members to interpret for the rest of the group their feelings about the selected poster. The leader may wish to ask if there are symbols in the posters that represent either implicitly or explicitly a kind of focal point for the emerging culture. If it seems natural or relevant, pursue a discussion of either a symbol that is in conflict within the culture (such as the flag) or a discussion of the peace symbol.

Suggestions for the leader: It should become clear that there is no right or wrong interpretation of the posters; they are simply works of art that allow for a variety of responses and interpretations. The leader should be particularly attuned here to letting controversy and conflict develop in the discussion of the posters. The material included in Chapter V and the discussion of some of the specific posters may be useful in developing certain themes and motifs in the midst of this discussion.

As a supplement to the poster art in this session on symbolism, the leader may wish to focus also on the music of the emerging culture. Refer to the suggestions for using Kathy Gregory's records cited in Session IV. However, the emphasis at this point would be on the symbolic import of the songs. Utilizing Kathy's music might be an option for a group that chose to show the film *Why Man Creates* in the session on creativity.

The aim of Session Four is to expose people to art forms with which they may not be particularly familiar and also to develop some sensitivity and awareness of the symbols for what it means to be human within a community.

Session Five. Art Project—A Form of Symbolic Expression

If the confrontation is conducted in a one-day session, the group may now need a more active kind of break from the emphasis on discussion. Therefore, the fifth Session could constitute an aesthetic project which in some ways might summarize and combine all the motifs so far considered. The creating of a mural can be experiential, stress subjective involvement, constitute a creative event, have a mysterious element, focus on symbolic communication, and because it is a communal act, be a precursor to the next session.

In preparation for this session the finger paints in four or five basic colors should be made beforehand and each color divided into two equal parts. The paper, about two or thrèe feet wide and about twenty feet in length, should then be taped to several long tables or even to the floor.

Divide the participants into two groups, perhaps by counting off, and ask them to go into separate parts of the room (two different rooms is even better) to create a mural. Each mural is to be fashioned communally, and the group is to decide how it wants to proceed. The mural is to be created in the medium of finger painting, which is a very sensual form of aesthetic artistic expression. The two groups, each of which should be divided relatively equally between the adults and young people, should attempt to express symbolically in their murals what their participation in this confrontation has meant to them.

The respective groups should then be given about twenty or thirty minutes to complete their creation. Play records for both groups while they are painting. For one group, play some hard rock, keeping the volume at a moderately high level. For the other group, supply classical music, perhaps piano concertos. This musical accompaniment to the creative act should be supplied unannounced by the leader so that later the groups can observe whether the music had any noticeable effect on their experiences, and if so, what the effect was.

After the two groups have completed their murals and cleaned up, call them all together again. Place the two murals on the floor, and sit in a circle around them. Then ask one of the members to walk along and tell what he sees in the mural created by the other group. Ask a second person to do the same with the other mural. This should take only a few minutes. Then proceed by asking the respective groups how they went about planning and creating their murals. Encourage individuals within the whole group to speak about their own contributions. The conversation should then focus around the symbols, images, and experiences that have been important for the group and that are likely to be quite evident in this activity. The leader should be sensitive to predominant themes and raise these up for the group's consideration.

The respective groups should be asked whether people tended to "do their own thing" by creating a symbol or design on one section of the mural. If the latter is true, as it usually has been in my experience with groups, this may lead to a discussion of the meaning of communality.

Session Six. Revitalization of Community

Probably no single desire is more readily expressed in American culture today than for community or a sense of unity. Also, few subjects are more controversial than the establishment of co-ed communes by members of the counter culture. These are experiments in new forms of community and alternative life-styles. This session, raising the issue of revitalization of community, might be initiated best by engaging in a role-playing situation.

The leader may request volunteers to participate in the role-playing. Select from those who volunteer, or, if none do, choose two men and a woman to be the subjects. The roles required are those of a father, a mother, and a son. The persons should be articulate and relatively free in expression. The age of the participants is not at this point an important consideration. Set the scene along the lines of my illustration in Chapter VI. The parents assume that their son, a college sophomore, will spend the summer at home, working in his father's business. However, in the course of the role-playing sequence the son announces that he plans to establish a co-ed commune in the Southwest.

Allow the role-playing scene to develop for five or ten minutes, as long as it is maintaining some kind of interest and movement. Interrupt on a high point by expressing appreciation to the group for being willing to share in this experience. This role-playing, although it may at times be amusing, is sometimes very painful for families who are caught in just such a confrontation—which is not always a constructive one. The participants might be encouraged to discuss the painful aspects of the scene.

The role-playing should then set the stage for a discussion of communality and its significance. Divide the group into three parts, perhaps by counting off. Ask this time that family units rearrange themselves so they are in the same small discussion groups. Indicate that you will provide each group with three questions for discussion, but that you will be giving them the questions one at a time. Provide the groups with the first question, and then assign each group to a discussion location. Move among the groups, helping them to focus on concrete experiences. Introduce the second and third questions when this is appropriate for each group.

The three questions are:

1. If the family is a form of community with which almost everyone has direct experience, and if it is ideally the place where there is real understanding, sharing, communication, and sensitivity, then what are the two characteristics of a really close family relationship? Suggest that the group discuss what really makes for a close family relationship either in your own experience or in families that appear to have this sense of communality. If the group selects general characteristics such as love, communication, or trust, they should give specific and concrete examples of how those characteristics are manifested.

2. If the family represents the ideal form of community (and it may not, since many of us may be unwilling to take the kind of risk and make the sacrifices that would allow for this kind of closeness), what are the two major impediments or problems that keep us from sharing such a close family relationship? Consider what the limitations are in ourselves, in other members of the family, or in the situation which make the realization of this sharing, openness, and trust so difficult.

3. The viewpoint should be shifted here, and the suggestion made to each group that perhaps the family relationship actually puts people into such close contact that they cannot have adequate perspective on a problem. Therefore, perhaps what they need is an extended family which will in fact facilitate the kind of experience that has been described in answer to the first question. Ask the group to imagine that you have invited them to join a family commune. Then provide an example of two models, perhaps utilizing the descriptions in Chapter VI. The leader could modify these illustrations to fit his own circumstances and those of the group.

Although there may be some point in having each group select a convener, it is not very useful to have the small groups report back. They will probably deal with their questions for thirty or forty minutes. The timing will depend on the leader, who should move from group to group interpreting and supplying additional questions. Reconvene to see whether anyone wants to reflect on the need for communality, or what aspects of the life of the particular sponsoring organization of the seminar might either contribute to or detract from a sense of communality. This may allow the discussion to get into a concrete evaluation of competitiveness, "duelogical" encounters, or the free expression of one's feelings. However, the discussion should be authentic to the group, and some groups may be much more capable of concretely evaluating this than others. The main aim is to open up new considerations for both the importance and the implementation of communality as a crucial factor in what it means to be human.

If the confrontation is being carried out in a one-day session, a rather vigorous break will be needed at this point. The leader may encourage the group to go outside if the weather allows, to participate briefly in some active form of recreation, or to relax and regain their momentum for the final session. A participant in one seminar described this as the "absorption" period.

Session Seven. Openness to Transcendence and the Future

During the course of Sessions Four through Six, particularly if these have occurred in a concentrated time span, the level of conflict may reach a peak; then the group will begin to develop lines of communication and reconciliation. The aim of this session is to consolidate any new avenues of communication, blossoming relationships, heightened awareness, or new insights. It is also a period to consider how the benefits or accomplishments of a seminar such as this could be implemented within the particular group or community in which the participants function.

To focus the discussion the leader might point out a recurring theme in the counter culture. The essential religious character of the emerging culture, which often ignores or rejects the established religious patterns and institutions, may be considered in terms of a radical openness to transcendence. This holds potential for reorienting the whole society to more humanizing values and goals. "Belief" in some form is essential to authentic human existence. Ask the participants:

1. What belief, if any, integrates and orients your own human experience?

2. Is a revival of commitment with a religious dimension becoming characteristic of the cultural revolution?

3. If you respond positively to this question, what implications do you understand such a religious renewal to have?

The leader may then attempt to focus the discussion on some plans for the future which might implement the results of this confrontation. Consider such questions as:

1. What insights or benefits have you achieved from this experience of confrontation?

2. Can a concern for the experiential, creative, mysterious, and communal help form a bridge to a more joyful, creative, and responsible future?

3. Have the attempts to evaluate these themes and motifs been a means of reestablishing or enhancing lines of communication across the culture gap?

4. Can the confrontation experience be imple-

mented beyond the boundaries of this group? If so, how?

5. Is this type of experience useful for other members associated with the sponsoring organization and should it be recommended to other groups within the community?

Session Eight. Evaluating and Concluding the Event

The confrontation should conclude with some type of summarizing experience. The leader may want to make a short summary statement of his own at this point, perhaps incorporating some sense of the quest for a vision and the importance of that search. Where it is relevant and applicable to the group, a closing experience in addition to this statement often bears a significant impact.

For secular groups, the experience may be a process known as "gift sharing." This can most effectively occur in smaller groups, perhaps the same ones that discussed community in Session Six. Here members of the group decide to give "gifts" to one another. Each person selects one other member of the group to whom he would like to give a gift. The leader should take care here that everyone is involved in the process.

The gift-giving is an act that indicates some sense of community and commitment to another. It can serve as a bond for those who have shared in a common experience and perhaps glimpsed a common vision. The gift is often a symbolic one. It may be a gift of time over the next few weeks to get together and share with the person and build upon what has occurred here. It may be the gift of attention, where one promises to listen more carefully in the future when the other person is encountered and addressed. It may be an actual gift such as a book or a painting, a story, a poem, a piece of sculpture. Such a gift may actually be created by one member of the group for the other. It could even be another finger-painting creation. The gift may be that of affection, which is demonstrated by an embrace.

A concluding activity appropriate for a religious group is a simple worship service. It may be the act of Communion or of embracing one another and granting the "Peace of God." Should a Communion service be selected, the denominational requirements of those participating ought to be considered. Whatever activity you choose should be carried out simply and informally. It should emphasize the themes of joy and hope. Encourage the persons in the group to express to one another how they have felt about the experience and the event. The session might conclude with the singing of a song or hymn.

Or the group may want to take leave of each other with a greeting or by expressing in a few words to some particular person their appreciation for that person's contribution. Concluding the event may be symbolic of the experience of constructive confrontation. However, it must be an event authentic to the group. It cannot be superimposed or pressed upon the participants if the spirit of the emerging culture is to be maintained, for it emphasizes the intrinsic worth not only of every individual but of every group.

The leader may ask each participant to write for him, either in the final ten minutes of the seminar or in the next few days, a few lines of evaluation. (See section VII, "Evaluation," for a suggested form for this evaluation. If the experience of constructive confrontation is to be shared with others, this data would help a leader to know how to revise procedures and improve the experience for others.

If the confrontation is to be an enjoyable and constructive one, the experience itself must incorporate some of the motifs of the emerging culture. It should be informal, flexible, spontaneous, and free. The leader should listen to his colleagues and be guided by them while he serves as an enthusiastic enabler and facilitator of constructive confrontation. If the experience is genuinely successful, new visions do emerge. A young college student who had not attended church (the sponsoring agency for the event in which he participated) for two years, returned to give the seminar "a try" with his parents because they were having serious trouble communicating. In his evaluation he declared: "You know as a result of this encounter I really sat down and talked with Mom and Dad for the first time about what we really believed and felt. And I discovered we were not as far apart as I thought—farther than I would like—but there is hope. Man, the church can be groovy!"

Peace.

VII. EVALUATION

1. What is your overall impression of the event?

2. What were its strengths?

3. What were its weaknesses?

4. What did you hope to gain from the experience when you enrolled?

5. What is the most important thing you derived from this encounter?

6. Would you recommend this event or a similar experience to other groups?

Any additional comments:

Songs by Kathy Gregory

PREPARED FOR KILLING

There's a gun in the rack near my library bookshelf
  And a gun in the desk of my office at work.
There's a gun underneath the white shirts in my dresser
  And one tiny pistol in the medicine chest.

There's a gun in my briefcase for riding the subway,
  And a gun in the glove compartment of my car.
There's a gun buried under the clubs in my golf bag,
  For no one will ever find me unprepared for killing.

There's a gun for robbers placed under my pillow,
  And a gun for the riots by the front hall door.
There's a gun at the entrance to my new fallout shelter,
  With enough ammunition to last me for years.

There's a gun that I carry when hunting for pheasant,
  And a rifle that's accurate one thousand yards.
And under my belt there's a double-shot derringer.
  No one will ever find me unprepared for killing.

I've invested a fortune in self-preservation,
  Preserving the life that I hold very dear.
And if anyone else dares to threaten my future,
  I know how to use all the guns I have here.

Now don't get me wrong; I'm not a cold killer.
  I believe in the laws of my country and state.
But in times such as these when the enemy's everywhere,
  We must be ready before it's too late!

There's a gun for robbers placed under my pillow,
    And a gun for the riots by the front hall door.
There's a gun at the entrance to my new fallout shelter
    Oh, no one will *ever* find me unprepared.

SPRING IN MY HEART

A yellow balloon. A big box of Cracker Jack.
    A walk in the zoo, a walk in the zoo.
A pigeon of gray, abobbin' his head
    As he struts along with you, along with you.

The clouds in the sky are chasing each other around,
    And laughing with glee, laughing with glee.
A cockatoo calls and suddenly all of the world's
    As right as can be, right as can be.

It's one of those times. A perfect Sunday.
    Spring is flirting with the tulips.
A little white sail. A frisky breeze.
    And someone's sailboat, painted blue, slips over the pond.

The fountain is bubbling up
    And sparkling high, sparkling high.
The shiny goldfish, their little gills open and close,
    Go wriggling by, wriggling by.

The funny thing is that this day happens whenever I want it to.
    I sit in my room. I close my eyes
And every time I think of you—
    A robin hops up, composing his warbling notes.
And right from the start, right from the start,
    I'm singing along enjoying the spring in my heart.

AFTER CAMBODIA

One rock falling on a mountainside is an avalanche.
One shot fired in a gathered crowd, stampede.
One chain broken in violence means more chains welded in war.
Blind force won't get us what we're looking for.

Any fear will breed more fear
   No matter how small it's born.
Any oppression is still oppression
   No matter which side you're on.
When violence is the strategy,
Then violence is the goal.
You can't build a new society
   With violence in control.

A rifle may seem the fastest way
   To get what we demand,
Yet the smoke from just one bullet
   Smothers what we've planned.
Then people begin an outcry
   For order at any cost.
When that's the promise leaders make and win,
   We all have lost.

If you would change the system's rules,
Don't play the system's game.
If you would build a freer land,
Let justice be your name.
If times of peace are to come about,
Then men of peace must appear.
The way to start is with yourself.
The time and place is here.

MYSELF

I'm following the wanderings of my mind, and it's a lovely trail
   to nowhere, out of nothing.
I'm looking for the self I never found along the road of life
   from nowhere into nothing.
So don't ask me to give up all my liberties,
And tie down my hands with responsibilities,
A floater's life is all I have ever wanted for myself,
   my own self, my beautiful self.

I'm worshiping the wonders of my mind and all its colors
   out of somewhere, into something.
The truest of realities is whirling in the color maze
   from somewhere, into something.

So don't trouble my head with technicalities,
Statistics, or scientific analyses,
The painless life is all I have ever wanted for myself,
   my own self, my beautiful self.

I'm doing just whatever strikes my fancy out of stimuli
   from anywhere, into anything.
I mustn't harm another human being breathing, eating,
   living anywhere, doing anything.
So don't ask me to fight your dirty wars for you,
To plan for the future or win a cause for you,
But loving life is all I've ever wanted
   for myself, my own self, my own self, my beautiful self.

IF

If I lie inside the covers
   with the darkened warm of breathing—only me,
And I curl up like a kitten,
   closing all the blankets very carefully,
Perhaps the goblins will not find me,
   will not touch me, maybe even go away.

If I climb onto a tree limb
   with the shiny leaves in bunches hiding me,
And I never move to stir them,
   sitting motionless and waiting quietly,
Perhaps the bullies will not find me,
   will not touch me, maybe even go away.

If I watch a funny movie
   with the lovely couples all surrounding me,
And I eat the salty popcorn and the candy
   till I'm laughing painfully,
Perhaps the worries will not find me,
   will not touch me, maybe even go away.

If I only talk politely
   to the friends who never fail inviting me,
And I skim the paper lightly,
   glancing at the news reports just casually,

Perhaps the questions will not find me,
  will not touch me, maybe even go away.

If I tumble in the grasses
  with another who pretends he's loving me,
And we exchange the little gestures,
  little phrases of the way love ought to be,
Perhaps the loneliness won't find me,
  will not touch me, maybe even go away.

If I lie inside the covers
  with the darkened warm of breathing—only me,
And I curl up like a kitten,
  closing all the blankets very carefully,
Perhaps my life will never find me,
  never touch me, maybe even go away, go away, go away.

CELEBRATION

In the midst of flashing neon darkness
  We dare this day to celebrate the light.

In the midst of blaring, shouting silence
  We dare this day to celebrate the word.

In the midst of bloated, gorged starvation
  We dare this day to celebrate the bread.

In the midst of bottled, bubbling thirst
  We dare this day to celebrate the water,

In the midst of smothered, gnawing doubt
  We dare to celebrate the affirmation.

In the midst of frantic, laughing death
  We dare this day to celebrate the life.

Let us sing, oh sing our alleluias,
Let us sing alleluia and rejoice,
Let us sing, oh sing our alleluias,
Let us sing alleluia and rejoice—
  with trembling.